Air Traffic Control

Control

Graham Duke

SECOND EDITION

LONDON

IAN ALLAN LTD

Contents

Cover:
The control tower at Bristol Airport.
Austin J. Brown/Aviation Picture Library

First published 1984
This edition 1986

ISBN 0 7110 1667 4

Published by Ian Allan Ltd, Shepperton, Surrey;
and printed by Ian Allan Printing Ltd at their works
at Coombelands in Runnymede, England.

1 Introduction

The aim of this revised and updated book
(the second edition) is to further explain the
arrangements for controlling the traffic in
the congested airspace of the United
Kingdom, with a particular emphasis on the
interest of enthusiasts. It should give
sufficient information and detail to enable
anyone with an involvement in aviation to
appreciate and understand the basics of a
system which is very sophisticated but at
the same time is basically simple in
approach. The only contact point between
the enthusiast and the actual world of ATC
is through an airband radio which is
capable of receiving voice transmissions
between aircraft and ground controllers. In
the last two years the number and
availability of such receivers has increased
considerably and many specialists are
appearing in the market to take advantage
of the expanding hobby of aircraft tracking.
Some of the lower priced sets give an
adequate return for your money, but with
so many improvements in the newer
receivers there is no doubt that it is well
worth purchasing a quality product to
obtain the best results.

In this first chapter a broad outline of the
system is given while later chapters are
devoted to expanding each particular
aspect. What the book does not do is
provide information on aircraft, airports or
flying skills. There are many excellent
books already available which adequately
cover these subjects, therefore there seems
to be little point in adding more.

This book, however, concentrates almost
exclusively on the intricacies of air traffic
control and in particular explains broadcast
messages heard on an airband radio
receiver.

The body responsible for the air traffic
control system in the United Kingdom is
the Civil Aviation Authority which was
formed in 1971. The CAA is responsible
jointly with the Ministry of Defence for the
National Air Traffic Services (NATS).
Approximately 75% of CAA staff are
employed by NATS.

National Air Traffic Services, which was
set up in 1962, is a joint civil and military
organisation responsible for the 'safe,

orderly and expeditious flow of air traffic within United Kingdom airspace'. The area of cover is approximately 350,000 square miles. Roughly half the staff employed by NATS are engaged on telecommunication systems, radars, landing and navigation aids and related facilities. The remainder consist mainly of civil and military air traffic controllers. Other bodies concerned with civil aviation are the United Nations agency ICAO (the International Civil Aviation Organisation) set up in 1944, which sets the standards of international flight safety and technical matters, and the trade association for airlines which operate scheduled services, the International Air Transport Association (IATA). This body is concerned with fares, baggage, cabin spaciousness and other related matters.

Airports are known by four letter codes under the ICAO system, and this code is the one used in flight plans and on radar. They are also identified by a separate 'ticket' code, consisting of three letters, under the IATA system, and passengers' baggage is labelled accordingly. London Heathrow, for example, is known both as EGLL (ICAO) and LHR (IATA).

There are two forms of airspace in the UK region, controlled and uncontrolled. Uncontrolled airspace covers large areas of the country in which aircraft may fly as they wish subject to certain simple rules. Cutting through these regions of uncontrolled airspace are protected corridors of controlled space, known as airways, come under mandatory control from ground stations. In addition, every airport is protected by a zone of controlled airspace, and where groups of airports occur, or where there are major airways intersections, these zones are grouped together to form Terminal Areas.

Special Rules Area

Above flight level 245, although the airspace is not officially controlled airspace, aircraft are still under positive control. It is known as a 'Special Rules Area'.

Radio Beacons

Navigation along the airways, and in other areas of controlled airspace, is accomplished by means of radio 'beacons' sited at strategic points. Aircraft are able to receive radio signals from these beacons, enabling them to track along the airways.

In addition to radio beacons, many aircraft use modern navigational computers which are extremely sophisticated, enabling aircraft to navigate with a high degree of accuracy without reference to ground based equipment. Approaches and landings at airports are also assisted by special transmissions from ground facilities.

Control Centres

Aircraft at or near airports are controlled by personnel at the particular airport. Shortly after an aircraft leaves the area of the airport, however, and joins the airways, the responsibility for control passes from the airport to one of two main Air Traffic Control Centres, situated at West Drayton (a few miles north of Heathrow Airport) and Prestwick in Ayrshire, known respectively as 'London' and 'Scottish'.

The London centre covers all airspace up to 55° north (roughly level with Newcastle) and the Scottish centre covers the region north of 55°. At Manchester International Airport there is a sub centre for West Drayton which handles traffic in the Manchester area up to 13,000ft.

The whole of the UK region, whether it be controlled or uncontrolled airspace, is sub-divided into 'sectors' for control and radio frequency allocation purposes.

Controlled and uncontrolled areas have separate radio frequencies, and in addition there are some situations where frequencies are split according to height. This means that high level and low level airways within the same sector may have separate radio frequencies. Airports and terminal areas also have individual frequencies.

For voice communication purposes civilian air traffic uses VHF radio wave bands with several hundred available channels, messages being transmitted and received on the same frequency.

London ATCC

The largest of the two UK air traffic control centres is at West Drayton, a few miles north of Heathrow.

Control of the London Flight Information Region (FIR) sectors takes place from the Operation Room, where a number of separate control suites are set out. The centre provides a continuous service with five shifts (known as 'watches'), with a total of more than 400 air traffic control officers and 200 assistants. On average, more than 2,400 separate flights every day are handled by West Drayton.

Above:
Air Traffic Radar Controllers at work. *Hollandse Signaalapparaten BV*

Left:
ATC training in progress at Bailbrook College, Bath.
International Aeradio Ltd

Above right:
A Plessey radar used for Air Traffic Control. *International Aeradio Ltd*

Right:
Using an optronic light pen in conjunction with computer controlled radar.
Hollandse Signaalapparaten BV

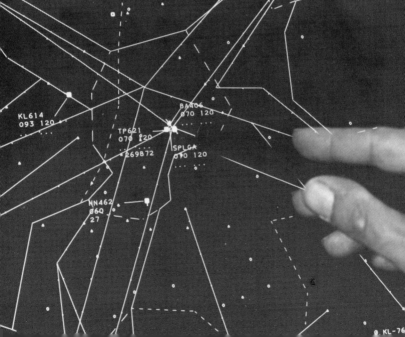

For every flight using controlled airspace, a flight plan will be filed giving details of the proposed flight. The information is held on computer until shortly before the flight enters the London FIR sector, when a 'Flight Progress Strip' is printed. This provides the controllers with details of the flight on a thin cardboard strip, mounted in a plastic holder, displayed in order on a panel at the controller's suite. Strips of various colours are used to give rapid identification of flights of different direction (eg eastbound, westbound, etc).

As each flight comes within the jurisdiction of a particular sector team, the flight progress strip is marked to indicate the various instructions and authorisations passed to the pilot. The controller issuing the instruction marks the strip as the words are being spoken, so that possible mistakes are avoided.

Radar

Radar is used at each control suite to monitor the progress of flights. The radar screen displays a map of the airways and reporting points for the particular sector, plus, of course, the positions of aircraft within radar range. In addition, aircraft equipped with a transponder are interrogated by a radio signal for an identification 'squawk', which is then shown alongside the aircraft position. The identity 'label' shows the aircraft call-sign, height and destination. The radar receiving stations, and the VHF radio transmitters, are located in various parts of the UK, the signals being passed between the centre and the remote stations by land line.

Radar and radio transmissions are continuously recorded and held for a period of 30 days in case there is any need for investigation of any particular incident.

It will be appreciated that the systems and the technology in use today for air traffic control are highly complex and sophisticated and only the briefest cover can be given in a book of this size.

Transmissions

The actual transmissions to aircraft in flight are arranged to ensure that an adequate signal strength is available in any particular sector, so that a flight will have no difficulty in receiving air traffic control instructions. This means that the actual transmitters may be located perhaps hundreds of miles

from the control centre, depending upon the sector concerned.

Similarly, transmissions from aircraft are picked up at remote receivers and then passed by land line to the control centre, both in respect of radar and radio.

At each air traffic control centre there are special radar displays, covering every sector of UK airspace, and these enable controllers to monitor the progress of air traffic through their areas. To assist them in this task, suitably equipped aircraft feed flight information details to the radar screens indicating the aircraft's identification, height and destination.

As a flight crosses from one sector to the next, or to airspace controlled by a different centre, the aircraft radio is retuned to the new frequency advised by the ground controller. Similarly, an aircraft intending to land at a UK airport would be instructed to contact the airport area control on the appropriate frequency. It is a fundamental rule of air traffic control that transfer of control must only take place if the transfer has previously been co-ordinated.

Separation

UK airspace is generally congested, especially at peak periods, with a high proportion of the traffic either climbing or descending. The controller's task is to ensure that flights are able to operate speedily and economically, with due regard for safety.

The controller must at all times keep aircraft apart by prescribed limits. Flights under radar control are not permitted to pass within five miles of each other if at the same height. This distance may only be reduced if the two aircraft are at least 1,000ft apart vertically, up to 29,000ft. Above 29,000ft the vertical separation required is increased to 2,000ft. In addition, depending on the heading of the aircraft, cruising levels are allocated in accordance with the 'semicircular rule', although ATC are able to authorise flight levels which do not comply with the rule.

Above Flight Level 450, separation between supersonic flights and any other aircraft is increased to 4,000ft.

Control

The actual 'control' takes the form of spoken messages transmitted between aircraft and ground stations, in which flight conditions, positions, flight levels and forward estimated times are provided by the aircrew, and instructions for changing direction, height and speed are passed to the flight by ground control who are usually assisted in their task by sophisticated radar techniques. A great deal of transmitted messages can be heard by the amateur with an airband radio and in favourable locations the range can easily be in excess of 200 miles where high flying aircraft are concerned.

Departure Flow Regulation

The volume of air traffic leaving UK airports is such that European airspace is frequently congested to the point where some restriction must be imposed on the flow of aircraft. This is implemented by a team of controllers in the Departure Flow Regulation section of the air traffic control centre.

Limits are placed upon the number of flights permitted to leave individual airports to ensure that the air routes of other European countries do not reach a level which exceeds their capacity.

Traffic Density

Civil aviation, in common with other forms of transport, has slack periods and 'rush hours' during the day, and the time chosen to listen to an airband radio will have a significant effect on the amount of traffic heard.

Because of the need to reduce aircraft disturbance to a minimum, night flights are severely curtailed, and most 'movements' in the UK occur during the day.

Almost all scheduled passenger flights from America and Canada arrive in Europe during the early morning, a convenient time for passengers and airlines alike, enabling aircraft to be 'turned around' in a few hours in readiness for the return transatlantic journey. From around 5am every day flights from America and Canada start to enter UK airspace, arriving on one of the North Atlantic tracks at one of the oceanic entry/exit points.

In most cases, flights from the eastern seaboard and the Caribbean arrive via routes which take them across south-west England, Southern Ireland and South Wales or Northern Ireland and North Wales, routeing either to UK airports or in transit to other European destinations.

Flights from the west coast of America and Canada generally cut across the UK from north to south, entering UK airspace in the Scottish Flight Information Region.

Arriving traffic builds up to a peak around 9am, hence the relatively high rates charged at Heathrow for aircraft arriving at this busy time. Connecting with these flights, the short haul traffic to and from European and United Kingdom destinations get under way during mid-morning, interspersed with other long-haul international flights and holiday traffic.

Later in the morning, at around 11am, the transatlantic traffic, which had arrived earlier that morning, starts to depart. These aircraft from European and UK airports meet in UK airspace, en route for their oceanic entry points, and by mid-day the busiest period of the day is under way. Every transatlantic flight will be in contact with the Oceanic Control Centre at Prestwick (except those which are departing from airports near the oceanic boundary, when oceanic clearances are given before the flight departs) on one of the two frequencies currently in use. Provided your receiver is on reasonably high ground, at least some aircraft requesting oceanic clearances can be heard anywhere in the UK.

By about 3pm, transatlantic traffic will have diminished considerably, although, of course, there will always be a number of flights to and from America and Canada which are outside the busy periods.

The late afternoon and early evening is mainly occupied by short haul flights again, with a fair number of charter holiday flights.

Light aircraft can be heard at any time during the day, especially when flying conditions are favourable, with weekend flying particularly popular.

In the later part of the evening, holiday flights are the main ones heard, with few long haul flights. In addition, because the traffic density is low, there is a reduced need for ATC transmissions, therefore it is less likely for any messages to be heard during such periods.

It is quite common for aircraft to fly considerable distances through UK airspace (perhaps 200 miles) when the airways are quiet, without a word being spoken between the aircraft and the ground.

High flying jet aircraft can be seen from the ground without difficulty, up to 30 miles away, particularly if vapour trails are being produced from the aircraft engines. There is, however, no guarantee that all aircraft will leave trails, and there are many periods during the year when there is no apparent indication of high flying traffic. Most aircraft will be following airways routes, but as the airways are 10 nautical miles in width the aircraft will often be on flight paths which vary considerably. In addition, as airspace above 24,500ft is under control, many aircraft will be on routeings which take them many miles away from the airways centre lines. Once the airways positions are known, with the aid of radio navigation charts, it becomes much more easy to spot air traffic.

To assist those concerned with aviation and air traffic control there are a number of special charts giving up-to-date details of airways, navigation facilities, restricted areas, radio frequencies, and so on. These are updated frequently and are generally available to the public at a surprisingly low cost. Although possession of such charts is not absolutely essential, the casual radio listener will find it extremely difficult to understand transmissions unless he or she is able to refer to such information. In any case, these charts are complex and fascinating in themselves, and anyone with an interest in aviation will find them absorbing documents.

North Atlantic

A considerable volume of commercial air traffic from UK airports crosses the North Atlantic every day. In addition, a large number of flights from other European countries also transit UK airspace to and from the American continent. Many of these can be seen and heard as they route across most parts of the United Kingdom. There are several North Atlantic routes to choose from every day, known as 'tracks', with an air traffic control centre situated at Prestwick in Ayrshire, Scotland. Aircrew speak to this centre as they fly through UK airspace, requesting clearance to use the particular track of their choice.

Information Services

Certain information is broadcast on radio frequencies within the airband range, using pre-recorded tapes, some on a continuous basis throughout the day and night and some for limited periods, usually confined to certain daytime hours. Most information relates to weather details for United Kingdom and some European airports, details of arrival and departure runways at

major airports, and details of daily air routes over the North Atlantic.

Eurocontrol

Aircraft using UK airports are subject to prescribed fees, laid down by the airport authority, varying according to the time of day, the weight of the aircraft, the number of passengers and so on. Part of the charges also relate to the air traffic control service provided by the airport.

After departure, a flight in UK airspace becomes liable for a charge in respect of the service provided by the appropriate air traffic control authority, not only of the UK but also of a number of other European countries through whose airspace the flight takes place. These charges are assessed according to a formula devised by Eurocontrol, whose headquarters are in Brussels, and each carrier eventually receives an account itemising every flight and the appropriate charge.

Conclusion

This concludes the general outline of the UK air traffic control system. Each of the remaining chapters expands individual aspects and should enable the reader to understand the principles. Because the book is written with the non-professional in mind, I have tried to explain ATC as simply as possible but without omitting any of the essentials.

It would have been impossible for me to embark on such a task unless I had been able to tap the knowledge of many individuals in the aviation world, and I wish to record my gratitude to them for their patience and their assistance. Any mistakes which might have crept into the book are probably due to my misunderstanding the situation rather than having been given incorrect information. Those who have helped are acknowledged at the end of the book.

One final point to remember is that the business of air traffic control and aviation is, by its very nature, subject to frequent changes, some minor and some quite fundamental. It is impossible to produce a publication of this type which can be guaranteed to be correct in every detail by the time it is published.

It is by no means unusual, when listening to an airband radio, to hear call-signs, reporting points, frequencies and so on that may not have been heard before. New

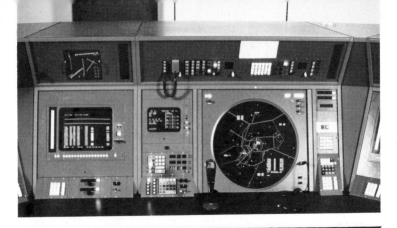

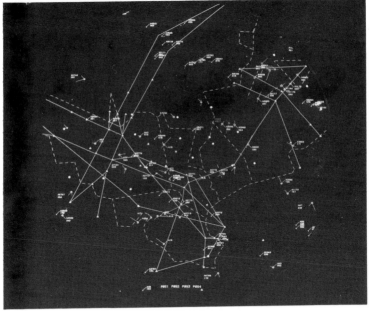

Top:
A modern ATC radar control suite.
Hollandse Signaalapparaten BV

Above:
One of the latest radar displays generated synthetically in four colours on a 23in cathode ray tube.
Hollandse Signaalapparaten BV

radio beacons are commissioned from time to time, new airways are sometimes brought into use, and changes in radio frequency are not uncommon. Even radio navigation charts are revised perhaps a dozen or more times every year, so that keeping right up to date can be expensive.

Nevertheless, I hope this book will at least serve as an introduction to the fascinating world of air traffic control, and that you will find it of some benefit.

2 Division of Airspace

Introduction

United Kingdom airspace is divided into two distinct categories, controlled airspace and uncontrolled (or free) airspace.

To ensure a safe and effective control system, sections of airspace around airports, both civil and military, and around major areas of intense activity, are protected by arranging them into various categories. No aircraft are permitted to enter such areas without authorisation. Connecting these areas are corridors of airspace, known as airways, each with specified upper and lower limits.

Outside these areas of controlled airspace aircraft may fly where they wish, without mandatory control, provided they comply with a set of simple rules.

Control of the immediate aerodrome area is the responsibility of the aerodrome controllers whereas airspace away from such areas is controlled by separate air traffic control centres.

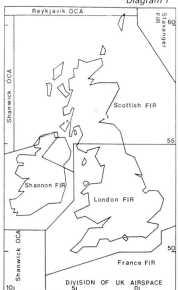

Diagram 1

Division of UK airspace showing the London and Scottish Flight Information Regions.

Flight Information Region

This is the whole area under the jurisdiction of a control centre, abbreviated to FIR, for low altitude airspace. Above 24,500ft the region is known as an Upper Flight Information Region, abbreviated to UIR. The perimeter of an FIR/UIR is known as the boundary.

United Kingdom airspace consists of two Flight Information Regions, with separation between the two at latitude 55° north. The Scottish Air Traffic Control Centre at Prestwick covers the Scottish region (Scottish FIR) including Northern Ireland, and the London Air Traffic Control Centre at West Drayton covers England and Wales, (London FIR). Southern Ireland is controlled by the Shannon Air Traffic Control Centre. Surrounding UK airspace to the south and east are the regions of other European countries, and to the north and west the ocean areas are controlled by Reykjavik Oceanic Control and Shanwick Oceanic Control respectively.

At Manchester there is an Air Traffic Control Sub-Centre which deals with traffic below 13,000ft in the Manchester area.

Controlled Airspace

As the term suggests, consists of areas in which aircraft are obliged to receive a control service from air traffic controllers located at air traffic control centres or at aerodromes. Aircraft are prohibited from entering controlled airspace without authority from air traffic control. Pilots are required to have certain qualifications and their aircraft must be fitted with specified navigation equipment. Flight plans must be entered for aircraft intending to fly in controlled airspace.

Special Rules Zones (SRZ); Special Rules Areas (SRA); and Control Zones (CTR)

These are terms which refer to sections of airspace surrounding and protecting military and civil aerodromes. Special Rules Zones and Control Zones extend from ground level to specified upper levels and Special Rules Areas extend from lower levels to upper levels specified on charts for each aerodrome. It can be seen that, in the case of Gatwick, the control zone embraces the immediate vicinity of the airport. Beyond the CTR, the airport is protected by the Special Rules Area, extending from 1,500ft to 2,500ft altitude, and this in turn falls within the London TMA, extending from 2,500ft altitude to 24,500ft flight level. Above 24,500ft is a Special Rules Area and the high altitude airways system.

Military Air Traffic Zones (MATZ)

These protect the immediate vicinity of military airfields, extending from ground level to specified upper limits.

Terminal Areas (TMA's)

These are blocks of airspace designed to protect groups of adjacent aerodromes and major intersections of airways. In the UK region there are Terminal Areas at London, Manchester, Belfast and in Scotland the Scottish Terminal Area contains airports at Prestwick, Glasgow and Edinburgh. A map illustrating the TMA's is shown in diagram 2.

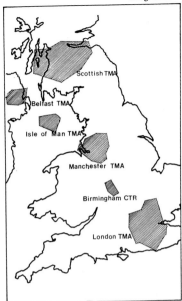

Diagram 2

Above:
The United Kingdom TMA's.

Below:
Part of the London Terminal Manoeuvring Area (TMA) showing the area around Gatwick Airport, taken from the Standard Terminal Arrival Chart. *Civil Aviation Authority*

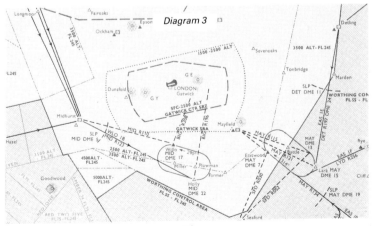

Diagram 3

11

A typical Air Traffic Control Operations Room. *Ferranti*

Left:
Ferranti ATC console position. The background shows a standard Air Traffic Tote showing NOTAM information.
Ferranti

Right:
Ferranti Computer Systems consoles for the Ministry of Defence and the Civil Aviation Authority as part of a radar processing and display system. The low overall height of the console affords a comfortable working position with easy reference to wall-mounted maps. *Ferranti*

Below:
A Sector suite at the London Air Traffic Control Centres West Drayton.
CAA

TMA boundaries are often irregular in shape, with lower levels which vary at different points according to traffic requirements. The London TMA, shown in diagram 3 has a number of subdivisions with differing lower levels, most of which are around 5,000ft. The upper level is 24,500ft for the whole area. The levels are arranged to coincide with the various airways which connect with the terminal area.

Airways

These are corridors of airspace 10 nautical miles in width, connecting with terminal areas or crossing the United Kingdom to connect with airways systems of adjacent control centres. Airways are all in straight lines between reporting points. They are classified as high altitude or low altitude, although this term may be misleading in some circumstances. The division between 'low' and 'high' occurs at 24,500ft, low altitude being below and high altitude above. Low altitude airways have specified lower flight levels which vary from around 4,000ft to as high as 20,000ft. A 'low' altitude airway may therefore occupy the space between 20,000ft and 24,500ft. Details of airways are given on radio navigation charts which are discussed in detail in chapter 5.

High altitude airways have a lower level of 24,500ft, and extend upwards to 66,000ft. They are prefixed with the letter 'U' for upper. Lower altitude airways, however, have no prefix. Lower and Upper airways with the same designation may not necessarily be on the same centre line. That is to say, the Upper airway may not be directly above the lower airway of the same designation. Airway Red 3 and Airway Upper Red 3, north of London, have centre lines which are three nautical miles apart.

There are also situations where two separate airways join together and are on the same centre line. As an example, Amber 2 and Blue 3 are combined between Daventry and Brookmans Park.

Aircraft wishing to join an airway must obtain a 'joining' clearance from Air Traffic Control. This may be provided to flights before they depart from an airport, or may be obtained en route by aircraft outside controlled airspace. Aircraft may join the airway from the side, or by climbing into the airway from below. Similarly, aircraft departing controlled airspace may do so by leaving the airway on one side or the other, or by descending through the lower limit of the airway.

Below:
A scale drawing of a cross section through an airway.

		Diagram 4	
	Special Rules Airspace between 24500 and 66000 feet		
Free Airspace	24500' Airway 10 nautical miles wide 6000'		
Ground level			
Sea level ↑			

CROSS SECTION OF A TYPICAL AIRWAY (drawn to scale)

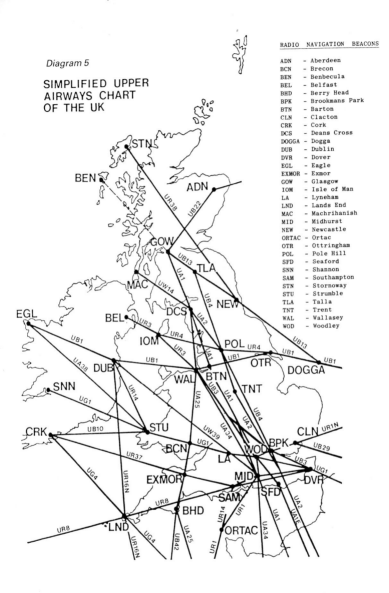

Diagram 5

SIMPLIFIED UPPER AIRWAYS CHART OF THE UK

Principal airways and navigation beacons of the UK, showing the South East/North West trend linking Europe with the North Atlantic.

Special Rules Area

This refers to all airspace between 24,500ft and 66,000ft. Aircraft operating within these levels are obliged to receive a mandatory air traffic service, and they are not required to remain within the confines of upper airways. Aircraft may route anywhere in the Special Rules Area provided ATC approval is obtained. Modern navigation equipment enables precise positioning without the use of VOR beacons, therefore routeings outside upper airways are commonplace.

Military Training Areas (MTA's)

These are blocks of airspace designated for the training and practice of military traffic. When such danger areas are 'active' civil traffic is prohibited from entering. It is common for some of these zones not to be used during the night or at weekends and aircraft may then be permitted to cross under ATC surveillance. In addition, some airways cross training areas but restrictions are placed on their use by specifying limitations as to times of operation; for example, by limiting their availability to 'weekends only' or by placing time limits on their periods of use.

Royal Flights

Whenever a civil or military aircraft carries a member of the Royal Family in the UK, an area of purple airspace is created which is intended to protect the Royal Flight throughout its journey.

Primarily, the members of the Royal Family are:

Her Majesty The Queen;
Her Majesty Queen Elizabeth The Queen Mother;
His Royal Highness The Prince Philip, Duke of Edinburgh;
His Royal Highness The Prince of Wales;
Her Royal Highness The Princess of Wales;
Her Royal Highness The Princess Anne;
His Royal Highness The Prince Andrew, Duke of York;
Her Royal Highness The Princess Andrew, Duchess of York;
His Royal Highness The Prince Edward;
Her Royal Highness The Princess Margaret.

However, it is also possible for other members of the Royal Family and for other Sovereigns and Heads of State to be included. Usually the Royal Flight will be routed along the normal UK airways system and through established control zones, and the airspace will then be declared Purple Airspace. When it is necessary to depart from controlled airspace, a Purple Airway, also 10 nautical miles wide, is established for the Flight. Similarly areas around airfields used by a Royal Flight will also be declared Purple Airspace.

The times allowed for Purple Airspace are from 15min before the arrival or 30min after the departure of the Royal Flight. The usual radio frequencies are used for a Royal Flight on a Purple Airway. Special ATC procedures apply in Purple Airspace to ensure separation from other flights.

Where members of the Royal Family fly by helicopter, a Royal Low Level Corridor (instead of Purple Airspace) is established, with check points at approximately 20 nautical mile intervals. A 10 mile zone either side of the helicopter's track is applied to military aircraft, and they must at all times be laterally separated by five nautical miles from the Royal Flight.

Uncontrolled 'Free' Airspace

This covers the remainder of the country's airspace, outside any of the control areas referred to earlier. It consists of lower airspace, which extends to about 8,000ft, and middle airspace, which extends to 24,500ft. As explained before, all airspace above 24,500ft is a Special Rules Area. (Remember also that there are no 'middle' airways. Airways below 24,500ft are 'lower', above 24,500ft 'upper'.)

Uncontrolled airspace is mostly used by light aircraft which are not equipped to operate in controlled airspace. However, this is by no means always the case. Some regular flights out of Heathrow fly in uncontrolled airspace to reach the provincial airport which is their destination. Any

Diagram 6

UK ALTIMETER SETTING REGIONS

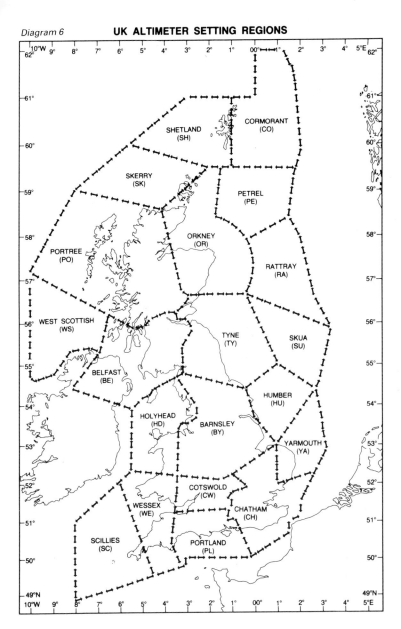

- SHETLAND (SH)
- CORMORANT (CO)
- SKERRY (SK)
- PETREL (PE)
- PORTREE (PO)
- ORKNEY (OR)
- RATTRAY (RA)
- WEST SCOTTISH (WS)
- TYNE (TY)
- SKUA (SU)
- BELFAST (BE)
- HUMBER (HU)
- HOLYHEAD (HD)
- BARNSLEY (BY)
- YARMOUTH (YA)
- COTSWOLD (CW)
- CHATHAM (CH)
- WESSEX (WE)
- SCILLIES (SC)
- PORTLAND (PL)

Altimeter Setting Regions (ASR's) in the UK. *Royal Air Force*

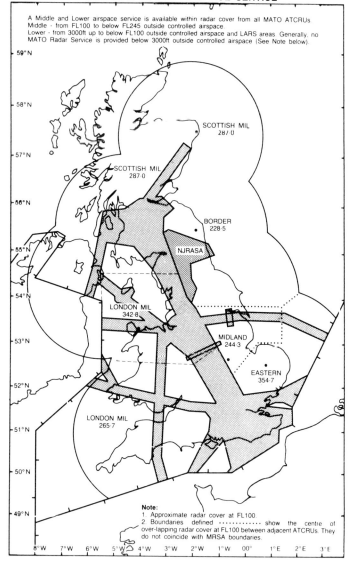

Diagram 7

MIDDLE & LOWER AIRSPACE SERVICE

A Middle and Lower airspace service is available within radar cover from all MATO ATCRUs.
Middle - from FL100 to below FL245 outside controlled airspace.
Lower - from 3000ft up to below FL100 outside controlled airspace and LARS areas. Generally, no MATO Radar Service is provided below 3000ft outside controlled airspace (See Note below).

59° N
58° N
57° N
56° N
55° N
54° N
53° N
52° N
51° N
50° N
49° N

SCOTTISH MIL
287·0

SCOTTISH MIL
287·0

BORDER
228·5

NJRASA

LONDON MIL
342·8

MIDLAND
244·3

EASTERN
354·7

LONDON MIL
265·7

Note:
1. Approximate radar cover at FL100.
2. Boundaries defined ············· show the centre of over-lapping radar cover at FL100 between adjacent ATCRUs. They do not coincide with MRSA boundaries.

8°W 7°W 6°W 5°W 4°W 3°W 2°W 1°W 00° 1°E 2°E 3°E

Above:
Map showing the range of cover of the UK Military Middle Airspace Radar Advisory Service.
Royal Air Force

Right:
Map showing the range of cover of the UK Lower Airspace Radar Advisory Service. *Royal Air Force.*

Diagram 8

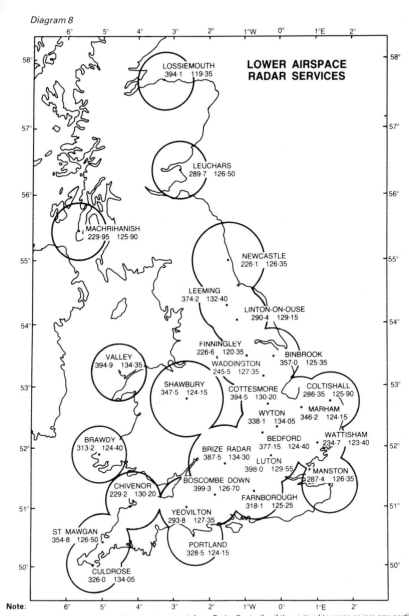

LOWER AIRSPACE RADAR SERVICES

LOSSIEMOUTH 394·1 119·35

LEUCHARS 289·7 126·50

MACHRIHANISH 229·95 125·90

NEWCASTLE 226·1 126·35

LEEMING 374·2 132·40

LINTON-ON-OUSE 290·4 129·15

VALLEY 394·9 134·35

FINNINGLEY 226·6 120·35

BINBROOK 357·0 125·35

WADDINGTON 245·5 127·35

SHAWBURY 347·5 124·15

COTTESMORE 394·5 130·20

COLTISHALL 286·35 125·90

WYTON 338·1 134·05

MARHAM 346·2 124·15

BRAWDY 313·2 124·40

BEDFORD 377·15 124·40

WATTISHAM 234·7 123·40

BRIZE RADAR 387·5 134·30

LUTON 398·0 129·55

MANSTON 287·4 126·35

CHIVENOR 229·2 130·20

BOSCOMBE DOWN 399·3 126·70

FARNBOROUGH 318·1 125·25

YEOVILTON 293·8 127·35

ST MAWGAN 354·8 126·50

PORTLAND 328·5 124·15

CULDROSE 326·0 134·05

Note:

1. Pilots receiving a service from Newcastle are to inform Radar Controller if they intend to cross or join any part of ADR DW11 within 30nm of Newcastle.

aircraft in uncontrolled airspace may take advantage of the country-wide Flight Information Service which is available on one of several frequencies listed in Chapter 12. Aircraft are not obliged to contact the Flight Information Service but the service is available for advice and information. It is not the same as being under control. Flights generally route from one aerodrome area to the next, taking advantage of the Flight Information Service in the uncontrolled airspace between aerodrome radar areas. The FIS offers information concerning weather, conflicting traffic, airport conditions, liaison between aerodrome control areas and clearances to join or cross airways. Since airways and TMA's have a lower level, aircraft may pass beneath them and remain in uncontrolled airspace. Aircraft in uncontrolled airspace have to comply with certain rules. Basically they must fly on a 'see and be seen' rule, or if weather conditions are unsuitable, on an instruments flying rule. They are known respectively as Visual Flight Rules and Instrument Flight Rules, abbreviated to VFR and IFR. More detail on these two terms will be found in chapter 4.

Lower Airspace Radar Advisory Service

This is a discretionary service provided by radar controllers at 27 civil and military aerodromes to aircraft in uncontrolled airspace within 30 nautical miles of the aerodrome flying at between 3,000ft and 9,500ft generally.

The service is advisory and not mandatory, therefore there may be aircraft in the area of which the controller may not be aware. The service is limited to the hours of operation of each participating unit, which may not be open at certain periods. There may also be limited service when aircraft are near the limit of radar cover. Aircraft will be given advice on conflicting traffic in the area. Also, aircraft must be flown in accordance with the quadrantal rule.

A map indicating details of the service is shown in diagram 8.

Aircraft flying in middle uncontrolled airspace between 10,000ft and 24,000ft may contact Middle Airspace Radar Advisory Service at one of eight military control centres when within range. A map of their locations is shown in diagram 7. Aircraft may receive advisory service to ensure a minimum of five nautical miles separation between aircraft at the same flight level which are known to the controller. However, as the service is not mandatory other aircraft may be operating in the same area unknown to the controller. The service may be limited when aircraft are flying near the limits of radar coverage. Aircraft must fly in accordance with the quadrantal rule.

Radar Services

Outside controlled airspace, civil and military Air Traffic Service Units are available (when conditions permit) to provide aircraft with advice and information. The services depend on controller workload at the time.

Radar Advisory Service provides a radar service which includes advice on other traffic which might conflict, with relative direction, distance, and required corrective action. The controllers will expect the aircraft to follow instructions on vectors or heights under Instrument Meteorological Conditions. If the pilot cannot comply with the controller's advice, or if he wishes to change level or heading, he should inform the controllers.

Radar Information Service provides pilots with details of traffic which might be expected to conflict, but avoiding action is not part of the service, although the controller may suggest repositioning. A radar information service may be provided when a radar advisory service is not appropriate.

Distress

Any pilot in difficulty or in urgent need of help whilst in flight may contact the Distress and Diversion Unit (D and D) at the Scottish and London Air Traffic Control

Right:
Positions of Radio Stations involved in the Emergency Fixer Service. The position of any flight transmitting on the Emergency frequency (May Day) is immediately plotted by this service. *Royal Air Force*

Diagram 9

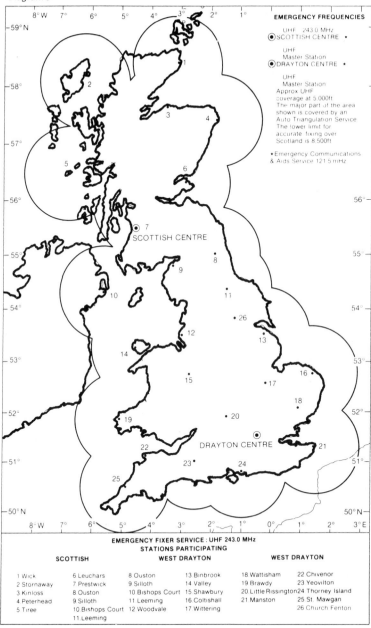

EMERGENCY FIXER SERVICE : UHF 243.0 MHz
STATIONS PARTICIPATING

SCOTTISH		WEST DRAYTON		WEST DRAYTON	
1 Wick	6 Leuchars	8 Ouston	13 Binbrook	18 Wattisham	22 Chivenor
2 Stornaway	7 Prestwick	9 Silloth	14 Valley	19 Brawdy	23 Yeovilton
3 Kinloss	8 Ouston	10 Bishops Court	15 Shawbury	20 Little Rissington	24 Thorney Island
4 Peterhead	9 Silloth	11 Leeming	16 Coltishall	21 Manston	25 St. Mawgan
5 Tiree	10 Bishops Court	12 Woodvale	17 Wittering		26 Church Fenton
	11 Leeming				

Centres on the VHF International Aeronautical Emergency Frequency (121.5MHz) which operates on a continuous basis. The call sign is *'Drayton Centre'* or *'Scottish Centre'* as appropriate. When a pilot contacts the D and D cell at either centre the position of the aircraft is determined by direction-finding equipment located at various stations in the UK (see diagram 9).

When a distress transmission is received on a frequency other than 121.5MHz, all other transmissions booome secondary. The distress transmission is top priority and all other stations on that particular frequency must be silent.

Where possible the distress traffic will then be requested to change frequency by the controller to 121.5MHz.

Initially, the distress call sign is *'Mayday'* (preferably spoken three times), and where possible the following details should be included in the transmission:

— Station being called;
— Callsigns;
— Aircraft type;
— Nature of emergency;
— Intention of the flight;
— Position, flight level and heading;
— Qualifications of the pilot;
— Number of persons on board.

Where a flight is in a condition of urgency (for example where the safety of an aircraft or a person is at risk), an *Urgency* message is to be transmitted using the word 'Pan-Pan' spoken three times. The same details as for Distress messages should be passed by the pilot.

Pilots with a lack of experience may use the word 'Tyro', so that controllers are aware of their limitations.

Pilots are at liberty to call the Distress and Diversion unit at either London or Scottish control to practice an emergency situation provided actual emergencies are not interfered with.

Air Traffic Control Designations

Aerodrome Control

This deals with the immediate vicinity of the aerodrome and gives authority for aircraft to land, take off and move around on the ground. The operations are undertaken from the glazed room at the top of the control tower, known as the Visual Control Room. London's Heathrow Airport, being such a large and busy airport, has correspondingly involved aerodrome control arrangements. The volume of traffic necessitates dividing the responsibilities for control between a number of personnel, each handling a specific section of the airport's traffic requirements.

Approach Control

This is applicable to aircraft within the area of the aerodrome as previously discussed. Aircraft are guided towards or away from the aerodrome either in preparation for landing, or to guide them on their route after departure. Traffic not intending to land is given an advisory service as it transits the area, to ensure there is no conflict with other aircraft using the airport or its surrounding area.

Area Control

This provides a service to aircraft using the airways or flying in the Special Rules Area. Most of the passenger and freight carrying aircraft in UK airspace route to their destinations under the surveillance of area control and for the amateur with an airband radio the majority of transmissions heard will be within this category. Military traffic using the airways also come within the jurisdiction of the civil air traffic control.

3 Airband Radios

Choosing a Radio

Strictly speaking, the receipt of broadcasts between aircraft and ground stations by unlicensed persons is illegal, although it is probably nearer the truth to say that making use of information obtained from such transmissions is what the law is trying to prevent. Certainly, it would not appear to the casual observer at an airport that anything illegal was taking place. The number of airband radios available and the inevitable groups of enthusiasts intently 'listening-in' might give the impression that no crime was being committed.

The comments and advice in this section, however, must be accepted on the basis that listening to ATC messages is illegal but the information is here to use in case the law is ever changed to allow harmless participation in this interesting activity. The other alternative, or course, is to try and arrange a visit to a local airport or, better still, an air traffic control centre.

Unfortunately buying an airband radio can be a risky business and it is all too easy to part with a considerable sum of money, only to find that the results are, at best, disappointing. One of the primary difficulties is that it is impossible to judge the quality of a radio in a high street shop simply because the surroundings are not suited to VHF reception. Similarly, listening to a radio on sale at, say, an airshow, may well be misleading because the test transmissions are likely to be from the local control tower, possibly only a few hundred yards away. As one would expect, such broadcasts will come through loud and clear and might well give the impression that the radio is a good buy.

A further point is that price is by no means an indicator of quality. The reception obtained by some radios, with a price tag in single figures, is truly remarkable, whereas it is not uncommon to find that other models, perhaps five times the price, and supplied by the same manufacturer, are of such poor quality that one wonders if there is an airband there at all.

If at all possible, try out a particular radio before deciding on a purchase, either by borrowing one or by talking to other enthusiasts who are already 'listening in'.

Some mail order companies operate on the basis that if the particular item they supply is not acceptable for whatever reason, it can be returned with no questions asked. Most catalogues have one or two airband radios so it is worth trying them. The different results obtained can be surprising.

Over the last few years the interest in 'airbanding' has increased considerably with the result that more and more radios are coming onto the market, and this can only benefit the enthusiast.

There are, of course, several specialist airband radio suppliers up an down the country, all of whom have a genuine interest in providing good advice and the benefit of their experience, and it is well worth paying one a visit if possible. Most of the periodicals on sale every week or month contain advertisements for companies who sell airband radios and their catalogues showing the range are available.

Airband radios vary tremendously in the range of facilities provided.

The simplest are merely small battery operated sets with continuous tuning provided with a 'short' scale covering the airways frequencies. In the middle range are larger sets, mains or battery operated, with a 'long' scale and possibly covering several other short-wave bands. At the top of the range are semi-professional sets, on which every frequency can be 'dialled' by selecting a set of frequency numbers, and also computerised sets which rapidly search through all frequencies, locking on to any transmissions which may occur.

With the cheap sets, with continuous tuning, there is no real separation between adjacent frequencies, so that the frequency selected may well be interrupted by other transmissions which are close by. For example, suppose that such a radio is tuned to a frequency of 132.60MHz. Because of the overlap of adjacent frequencies, transmissions broadcast between possibly 131.60 and 133.60 will be heard, assuming of course that the radio is in a suitable reception area. In this particular example, this means that all the following frequencies might be heard:

131.90	British Airways 'Company'
132.00	France Control
132.05	London TMA
132.20	Maastricht Control
132.60	London Control
132.80	London Control
132.82	France Control
133.45	London Control
133.60	London Control

The result of this is that there is a chance of any one of nine transmissions being received (given favourable conditions) rather than a single one.

This can of course be a disadvantage if the set is tuned to a particular frequency, because other messages can completely obliterate the transmission and this is frustrating when trying to listen to one individual aircraft. On the other hand, it is far more probable that you will at least hear some messages because so many frequencies are scanned in a very short space of time, whereas with a more sophisticated airband monitor the set will only receive transmissions on the specific frequency to which it is tuned, and this can often mean long periods of complete silence.

With cheap sets, interruptions by adjacent frequencies is known as 'heterodyning', and this is the result of poor design, and lack of selectivity.

More expensive sets, especially those with scanning facilities, have better receiver design and are narrow band. Better sensitivity allows reception over longer distances.

Many radios are available which are not exclusively airband, but cover several other ranges, such as marine band, long and medium wave bands, and two or three short wave bands. Such radios may not be a good buy, especially if only airband frequencies are required since a proportion of the cost will have been used in providing the other unwanted bands.

If all else fails, a final decision on which radio to buy can be made by visiting any of the large airports. On the public viewing areas there will undoubtedly be a number of enthusiasts with airband radios, and most will be delighted to show off their particular set. By comparing radios in such situations, one will invariably stand out above the rest.

If the radio is one which is battery operated only, a small transformer, of the type used for pocket calculators, can be purchased for a relatively small outlay (compared with the cost of replacement batteries) and the wires connected to the battery holder in the set, to enable the radio to operate on mains supply. This will not only save money but will give a consistent standard of performance without the deterioration which occurs when batteries start to run down.

If you are in doubt as to whether a particular set is suitable for use with a transformer, take specialist advice first, either from an electrician or from someone who understands the technicalities of radio.

In addition to the popular small receivers available in many shops, there are a number of various models of specialist receivers which vary in price and performance according to the specification of set.

A crystal controlled receiver with perhaps 12 crystals, and fitted with a built-in telescopic aerial and rechargeable batteries, is a typical model. The purchaser will need to specify the frequencies desired for each of the crystals. This, of course, has its limitations, firstly because only 12 channels can be received, and secondly it means that most if not all of those specific channels would not be appropriate if the receiver were to be used away from a home base. Furthermore, the purchaser needs to be aware of those radio frequencies most suitable for good reception and where area control is concerned the channels in use can vary during different parts of the day or at different times of the year and, of course, all transmissions could then be lost. Airports usually stick to the same frequencies for approach, tower, ground, etc so that there is less of a problem in those cases.

An alternative model is one with a combination of crystal controlled frequencies and a fully tunable scale for the full range of airband channels. With this type, the whole airband range can be searched manually, while a number of individual frequencies specified by the purchaser can be provided to give exact reception for those transmissions which are popular in the locality.

A further development is the receiver with a fully tunable scale and several crystal controlled frequencies which are scanned automatically by the set, 'locking' onto any transmission heard on any of those channels.

Top of the range within the VHF airband range is the synthesised monitor that is capable of pinpointing every one of the 720 airband channels, without the need for individual crystals. In addition, some sets can scan up to 100 stored frequencies automatically. Naturally with the more sophisticated receivers the sensitivity of the set is greater, and all have squelch control which cuts out interference and background noise.

Many sets have rechargeable batteries, or can be operated via a mains transformer, and many can be run from a car battery. Some sets require an external aerial, and others have either a built-in aerial or a combination of built-in aerial and external aerial provision.

It is important to obtain advice on the use of mains transformers for battery operated sets because a regulated power supply is essential if damage to the receiver is to be avoided. Changing to a transformer will of course prevent the use of the radio as a portable, so an alternative is to change to rechargeable Nicad batteries. Nicad batteries operate in a different way to normal dry cells, which start to lose their power as soon as they are manufactured, and receiver performance gets progressively worse. Nicad batteries, however, maintain the same high level of performance until the point in time when they quickly discharge.

Getting the best from your radio

Radio transmissions between air traffic controllers and civilian aircraft over the UK operate on VHF wave bands. Military aircraft using the 'airways' may also be heard, but other military traffic use UHF radio which is not covered in this book.

The lowest VHF frequency is 118.000MHz, and the highest 135.975MHz. The sub-division of frequencies is .025MHz (25KHz), commencing at 118.000, the next being 118.025, then 118.050, 118.075, 118.100, 118.125, 118.150 and so on. There are therefore 720 available channels in the range. In practice, UK frequencies are virtually all in 50KHz spacings (ie the second digit after the decimal point is either '0' or '5') meaning that only 360 channels are in use.

The airband frequency details given at the end of the book will show that the vast majority are in the 50KHz spacing. Those which are spaced at 25KHz are shown as ending with a '2' or a '7', because only the first five digits are quoted when referring to airband VHF frequencies. Thus 133.475 would be quoted as '133.47' and 123.225 as 123.22', the final 5 being omitted in both cases. Frequencies ending in '50' or '00' would also be quoted without the final zero (in the case of 50) or without the final two zeros (in the case of 00). For example:

134.450 becomes 134.45
123.950 becomes 123.95
118.550 becomes 118.55
but 132.00 becomes 132.0
129.600 becomes 129.6
and 119.200 becomes 119.2

When tuning in to a specific frequency on an accurate receiver with synthesised control it may often be found that the best reception is obtained at a point slightly higher or lower than the published frequency. For example, the Volmet South broadcast, published as 128.6MHz may in practice be found to be better at 128.595 (5KHz lower) or at 128.605 (5KHz higher) and this is particularly so when the area of reception is close to the limits of the transmitter.

Because the transmissions are VHF, they operate on a 'line-of-sight' principle. That is to say, signals will be received if the transmitter is in a direct visual line with the receiver, and not obstructed by hills, heavy buildings and so on. A radio receiver positioned on the side of a hill will be able to receive transmissions from high flying aircraft, but the reception from ground stations, airports, or low flying traffic which are shielded behind the hills will be of poor quality.

Radios positioned on high ground will be able to receive transmissions from high flying traffic 200 miles away without difficulty, which means that every part of the UK is suitable for receiving air traffic messages. Reference to 'high' ground does not necessarily mean locations which are well above sea level, but rather to positions which are the highest in the locality. For example, low lying areas such as Norfolk can be expected to be better reception areas than, for example, a position between hills in Wales, even though the latter may be considerably higher in terms of height above sea level.

It can be seen that there is no need to live near an airport in order to obtain good reception of ATC broadcasts, unless, of course, landings and take-offs are of particular interest. Also, being immediately under or alongside an airway is not particularly good for reception, which is usually distorted and difficult to understand because the aircraft is so close to the receiver. Clear and undistorted reception is usually obtained from aircraft at high altitude within a range of 100 miles of the receiver and given a good radio position 200 miles radius is quite acceptable.

The ATC transmitters are located around the country, for radar and radio, linked to the ATC centres at Prestwick and West Drayton. If you happen to be anywhere near a transmitter, the ATC messages from that particular transmitter will be easily received.

Reception will vary during the year, even though the radio is always on the same spot. It will usually be found that during conditions of fog, especially during autumn and spring, reception will be greatly improved due to the reflection of radio waves.

In such cases, messages not usually heard at all will be coming through loud and clear but the quality and range will gradually deteriorate as the weather improves.

In particular, the most dramatic improvement will be in the reception of ground stations, and messages broadcast from other European countries can often be heard in such conditions.

It will soon be noticed that at certain times some of the radio frequencies usually in use for airways control cannot be heard. This is normally only during quiet periods — for example, late evening or at weekends. The reason is that because of the reduction in traffic certain sectors are closed down and the flights normally under the control of that particular sector are then passed over to an adjacent controller who then assumes responsibility for both areas, although, of course, the traffic volume is within limits. For the airband listener this can be confusing, especially if a particular radio frequency which is normally very active suddenly becomes completely silent. Even more perplexing is the situation where the aircraft are broadcasting and receiving messages on one frequency, while the controller is transmitting on two

frequencies. For example, frequencies 133.7 and 134.75 handle airways traffic between London and the North of England on Airways UB4, UA2 and UA1. During quiet periods, frequency 134.75 is withdrawn and all aircraft are transferred to 133.7. ATC transmissions, however, are broadcast both on 133.7 and 134.75, with flights answering only on 133.7. This means that the controller can be heard transmitting on 134.75 but there are no replies. Later, of course, as traffic density increases, the 'unused' frequency will be brought back into operation, usually during the early morning. A radio channel which has been completely quiet will suddenly come to life as a number of flights are handed over to the new sector controller.

In addition to the frequencies quoted above, there are several others — for example 133.6 is replaced by 132.6, and 134.45 is replaced by 127.7, during quiet periods.

The opposite situation is also true. During very busy summer peak periods, the normal sectors may be sub-divided and new frequencies brought into use. From the airband listeners' point of view this means that traffic is under the jurisdiction of one controller for much shorter periods, although, of course, the number of flights is greater.

From the illustrations it is plain that height above sea level is of primary importance for long range coverage. Dramatic differences in reception are achieved by changes in level of perhaps only a hundred feet. To obtain the best results, and to establish the capability of a new radio, it should be taken to a high point. Choose a site well away from electricity power lines, telephone lines, other aerials or transmitters. These can seriously affect the quality of reception, and may even result in complete blank spots.

Stick a narrow piece of adhesive paper alongside the scale (118-136MHz), switch on the radio and move up and down the scale until a transmission is heard. Best results will be obtained during peak periods (see chapter 1). If there is an airway in the vicinity (say within 100 miles) an indication of the probable frequency for that airway will be stated on a radio navigation chart. Unfortunately, these frequencies are not always used in practice, so do not be surprised if some searching is necessary.

Another point is that many radios are not

properly adjusted during manufacture and it is quite possible that the position on the frequency scale will not coincide with the figures marked on the scale — in other words, if the pointer is set to (say) 127.00 the actual frequency heard might be 130.00 or 124.00. 'Setting-up' an airband radio, especially a lower priced model, is therefore a matter of trial and error. If there is an airport in the area, the transmissions can be heard without difficulty. A telephone call to the local airfield will soon establish the frequencies in use, and once a positive transmission has been picked up the position of that particular frequency can be marked on the adhesive label on the tuning scale. As far as reception is concerned, the quality inside a car is just as good as in the open air, although several positions can be tried to get the best results.

Placing the radio on top of the dashboard, with the aerial lying horizontally alongside the windscreen, is usually quite acceptable.

When using a radio for the first time there is naturally a desire to move up and down the scale, searching for messages. Although there is no harm in this, more knowledge of the activity in the vicinity will be obtained by leaving the radio tuned to one particular frequency. If this happens to be the frequency for an airway, a logical and consistent pattern of messages will begin to emerge. Aircraft will refer to specific reporting points, and will give headings and flight levels.

As aircraft pass from one sector to the next, the controller will advise the new radio frequency, whether it be under the same control centre, a terminal area, an airport, or an adjacent country's airspace.

By making a note of frequency changes, and especially if a radio navigation chart is available, it will soon be apparent that certain frequencies are more popular than others in a particular area.

It will be seen that, as a general rule, high flying aircraft will be using frequencies towards the high end of the scale (between 125.00 and 136.00) and low flying aircraft and airports will use those at the lower end.

As different frequencies are mentioned and transmissions received, their positions can be marked on the adhesive tape until eventually the whole range of frequencies from 118 to 136 can be indicated. This enables every frequency to be quickly and easily located. Of course, if the radio is one

fitted with frequencies which can be 'dialled' there is no problem in locating the various positions.

It will be advantageous to tape record some transmissions, at least until you have gained some experience, so that the recordings can be played back as often as wished. The words and phrases in use can be considered in far more detail in this way.

Gradually a pattern will be established. Aircraft entering the sector (for example) from the west, will state their position, next reporting point, flight level and perhaps heading. After passing through the sector the aircraft will be requested to contact the next sector. Similarly aircraft entering from the east, and perhaps the south and north, will follow set patterns until they are handed over to the next controller.

In most cases, only the aircraft will be heard. Because of the remote locations of transmitting stations, the ATC replies will not be heard unless the transmitter is in the vicinity. This is where height is so important — several ATC broadcasts may be heard on high ground, whereas none may be heard only a few hundred feet lower. If the transmitter is in the area, all messages will come through loud and clear.

There are a number of transmissions which are broadcast on the VHF band on a 'continuous' basis (note that these may not be operating for 24 hours but for certain specified periods. Details are shown in Chapter 12). These transmissions provide information to aircrew about weather, airports or transatlantic routes. By selecting the appropriate frequency aircraft can obtain direct information without talking directly to the controller.

A group of frequencies is available with the airband for use by airlines for non-control use, and these are known as 'company' frequencies. They are used for scheduling and other domestic purposes, and many airlines have offices at major airports. The majority of 'company' frequencies are around 130.00MHz to 132.00MHz although of course there are a few exceptions. British Airways at Heathrow, for example, use 131.9MHz. The use of company frequencies enables aircraft to contact their own organisation directly without the need to use the air traffic control system as an intermediary. Chapter 11 contains some details about company activities at airports.

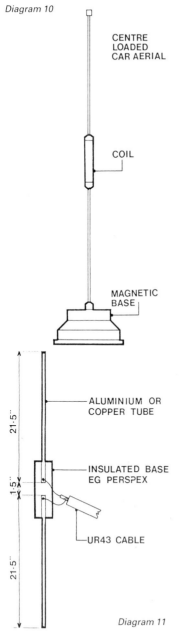

Diagram 10

CENTRE
LOADED
CAR AERIAL

COIL

MAGNETIC
BASE

21·5"

ALUMINIUM OR
COPPER TUBE

1·5"

INSULATED BASE
EG PERSPEX

UR43 CABLE

21·5"

Diagram 11

Whilst best reception is obtained on high ground, for practical purposes it is not possible to be in such a situation permanently. Much of the listening will take place at home, and there are a few points worth remembering to improve reception.

Although in theory reception should be better outside in the open air, it is possible to find situations where good results are obtained indoors. With a radio receiver fitted with a built-in aerial, it is important to experiment by moving the set around the house as considerable differences in range can be found. Sometimes good results occur when the aerial is close to an internal wall, or when the aerial is set at an angle rather than in the vertical position. Setting the receiver to one of the continuous broadcasts will help when trying to find the best spot for reception rather than having to wait for intermittent messages from aircraft in flight. The only other way to

Diagram 12

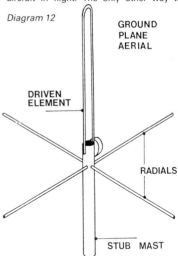

GROUND
PLANE
AERIAL

DRIVEN
ELEMENT

RADIALS

STUB MAST

Above left:
An aerial suitable for mobile use, with a magnetic base which is attached to a car roof.

Left:
A ground plane aerial suitable for airband receivers

Above:
A simple aerial for airband reception which can be easily made by the amateur.

28

improve reception at home or in the car is to provide a separate external aerial. Some of the more specialist sets are not supplied with an aerial, so one has to be provided in any case.

When the radio is to be used in a vehicle, a centre loaded magnetic type of aerial is ideally suitable and this uses the vehicle roof as part of the system. The aerial is connected to the set by a SO239 socket and PL259 plug if provision is made for this, or alternatively clipped to the in-built aerial, fitted to the set, by means of a simple metal clip. The built-in type of aerial must be in the closed position.

Car aerials are fixed to the vehicle either by a magnetic base, located in the central area of the roof, or by a similar aerial provided with a clamp which secures the aerial to the car gutter (diagram 10). A different type of aerial, known as a ground plane aerial, is used for fixed situations — that is, when the receiver is to be used at home. This design of aerial is shown in diagram 12, and several specialist airband dealers supply the ground plane aerial in kit form. Even so, height is extremely important, and the provision of a specialist aerial in a position which is either low-lying or surrounded by high ground can be very disappointing, although the results will undoubtedly be far better than those obtained without a specialist aerial.

The co-axial cable connecting the receiver to the aerial is also important.

Although ordinary television coaxial cable is acceptable, type UR43 (or equivalent) will give superior results. Cable type UR67 is

Below:
Map showing the positions of remote transmitting and receiving stations for the London FIR. *(Produced from information supplied by the CAA).*

Bottom:
The advantages of high ground for the receipt of ATC transmissions is illustrated in this diagram. A radio receiver at R1 will be suitable for high flying aircraft, but position R2 will enable low level flights to be heard clearly as well.

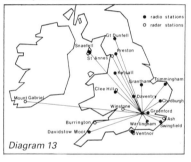

Diagram 13

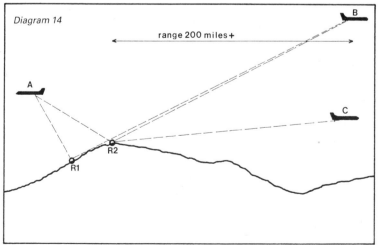

Diagram 15

better still but is less pliable. A simple type of aerial which is easy to make is shown in diagram 11. It consists of two sections of aluminium tubing of the lengths shown, fixed to an insulated base and connected to the radio receiver with UR43 co-axial cable. The central core of the cable is connected to the aerial (which is in the closed position) and the earth lead is connected to the radio casing, although in practice there is only a marginal signal loss if the earth is not connected to the receiver.

Alternatively, if the receiver is provided with an aerial socket a suitable connecting plug may be used. In all cases it is important to locate the aerial in a position which is high as possible, and it is also important to keep the length of connecting cable as short as possible.

Right:
Locations of new high powered Secondary radars recently installed in the UK.

Left:
Signal R537S airband tunable receiver with two crystal controlled channels. *Lowe Electronics*

Above:
AOR AR2002 Monitor receiver with many facilities in addition to airband frequencies. *Lowe Electronics*

4 Radio Telephony

The English language is used throughout the world for international air traffic control messages. It is essential that aircrew and controllers, especially those who are not English speaking, adopt an agreed procedure to ensure that words and numerals are clearly understood. As a basis, the English alphabet is represented phonetically as follows. In cases of doubt words are spelled out using this alphabet.

Letter	Word	Pronunciation
A	Alfa	*AL* FAH
B	Bravo	*BRAH VOH*
C	Charlie	*CHAR* LEE
D	Delta	*DELL* TAH
E	Echo	*ECK* OH
F	Foxtrot	*FOKS* TROT
G	Golf	GOLF
H	Hotel	HOH *TELL*
I	India	*IN* DEE AH
J	Juliett	*JEW* LEE *ETT*
K	Kilo	*KEY* LOH
L	Lima	*LEE* MAH
M	Mike	MIKE
N	November	NO *VEM* BER
O	Oscar	*OSS* CAH
P	Papa	PAH *PAH*
Q	Quebec	KEH *BECK*
R	Romeo	*ROM* ME OH
S	Sierra	SEE *AIR* RAH
T	Tango	*TAN* GO
U	Uniform	*YOU* NEE FORM
V	Victor	*VIC* TAH
W	Whiskey	*WISS* KEY
X	X-ray	*ECKS RAY*
Y	Yankee	*YANG* KEY
Z	Zulu	*ZOO* LOO

Numerals are pronounced in accordance with the following table:

0	ZE-RO
1	WUN
2	TOO
3	TREE
4	FOW-er
5	FIFE
6	SIX
7	SEV-en
8	AIT
9	NIN-er

Some of the main uses of the English language in air traffic control throughout the world are as follows. Much of what is explained is taken from the official publication on Radio Telephony (CAP 413) and those who wish to study the subject are advised to obtain a copy.

Thousands are transmitted by saying each numeral separately, followed by the word 'tousand'. For example, 15,000 is pronounced 'One Five Tousand'. 33,000 is pronounced 'Three Three Tousand'. (Special rules apply to 'Flight Levels' which are dealt with later.)

Other examples are set out below. Each numeral is pronounced separately.

27 is pronounced Two Seven;
99 is pronounced Nine Nine;
410 is pronounced Four One Zero.

Where decimals are involved, the word is pronounced 'Day See Mal', eg 'One Three Five Decimal Six'. In practice, the word decimal is frequently omitted. Especially where radio frequencies are involved, eg 135.6 is often spoken as One Three Five Six.

Messages are classified into types and priorities, as set out below:

1st priority — Distress messages, identified by the prefix 'Mayday';
2nd priority — Urgent messages, identified by the prefix 'Pan';
3rd priority — Messages concerning direction finding;
4th priority — Flight safety messages, including ATC messages and position reports;
5th priority — Messages concerning meteorology;
6th priority — Flight regularity messages (known as 'company messages').

All aircraft within the jurisdiction of a particular controller will receive transmissions from that controller, and in addition each aircraft will hear transmissions of all other aircraft in the sector on the same frequency. Before establishing contact with a sector controller, therefore, the aircraft must listen on the particular frequency to ensure that no other transmissions are taking place. Once this is reasonably certain the aircraft will attempt to contact the controller. When contact has been established, the text of the message is transmitted.

As it is essential that there is no risk of misinterpreting reports or instructions, information is given in precise terms by international agreement.

In the event of an aircraft failing to make contact, the pilot will return to the last frequency on which successful transmissions were made and explain that no contact can be established. The controller will then check with the next sector and possibly give the pilot an alternative radio frequency.

The 'readability' (ie the clarity of transmissions) is expressed in accordance with the following scale:

Readability 1 Unreadable;
Readability 2 Readable now and then;
Readability 3 Readable but with difficulty;
Readability 4 Readable;
Readability 5 Perfectly readable.

An example of the use of this scale is 'Sabena five four six London read you strength five. How me?'

The London Air Traffic Control Centre is calling Sabena 546, whose transmissions are perfectly readable. The controller is asking whether his messages are being received by the aircraft.

Certain abbreviations are often used in aviation terminology. The abbreviations annotated with an asterisk are normally spoken as complete words. The remainder are normally spoken using the constituent letters rather than the spelling alphabet.

ACC	Area control centre
ADF	Automatic direction-finding equipment
ADR	Advisory route
ADT	Approved departure time
AFIS*	Aerodrome flight information service
AFTN	Aeronautical fixed telecommunication network
AGL	Above ground level
AIC	Aeronautical information circular
AIP	Aeronautical information publication
AIS	Aeronautical information services
AMSL	Above mean sea level
ATC	Air traffic control (in general)
ATCC	Air Traffic Control Centre
ATD	Actual time of departure
ATIS*	Automatic terminal information service

ATS	Air traffic services
ATSU	Air Traffic Services Unit
ATZ	Aerodrome traffic zone
CAVOK*	Visibility, cloud and present weather better than prescribed values or conditions (CAVOK pronounced Cav-okay)
CTR	Control zone
DME	Distance measuring equipment
EAT	Expected approach time
EET	Estimated elapsed time
ETA	Estimated time of arrival or estimating arrival
ETD	Estimated time of departure or estimating departure
FIR	Flight information region
FIS	Flight information service
GMT	Greenwich mean time
H24	Continuous day and night service (H24 pronounced Aitch Twenty Four)
IFR	Instrument flight rules
ILS	Instrument landing system
IMC	Instrument meteorological conditions
MATZ*	Military Aerodrome Traffic Zone
MET*	Meteorological or meteorology
NDB	Non-directional radio beacon
OAC	Oceanic area control centre
OCA	Oceanic control area
PAPIS*	Precision approach path indicating system (PAPIS pronounced Pa-pee)
QDM	Magnetic heading (zero wind)
QFE	Atmospheric pressure at aerodrome elevation (or at runway threshold)
QGH	Letdown procedure using VDF equipment
QNH	Altimeter sub-scale setting to obtain elevation when on the ground
QTE	True bearing
RCC	Rescue co-ordination centre
RTF	Radiotelephone
RVR	Runway visual range
SID*	Standard instrument departure
SIGMET*	Significant information concerning en route weather phenomena which may affect the safety of aircraft operations
SSR	Secondary surveillance radar
STAR*	Standard (instrument) arrival route
TAF*	Aerodrome forecast
TMA	Terminal control area
UIR	Upper flight information region
VASIS*	Visual approach slope indicator

	system (VASIS pronounced Var-zi)
VDF	Very high frequency direction-finding system
VFR	Visual flight rules
VHF	Very high frequency (30MHz to 300MHz)
VMC	Visual meteorological conditions
VOLMET*	Meteorological information for aircraft in flight
VOR	VHF omnidirectional radio range
VORTAC*	VOR and TACAN combination

The following definitions are commonly used in ATC transmissions:

Aerodrome Control Service: Air traffic control service for aerodrome traffic.

Aerodrome Traffic: All traffic on the manoeuvring area of an aerodrome and all aircraft operating in the vicinity of an aerodrome.

Aeronautical Mobile Service: All radio communication service between aircraft stations and aeronautical stations, or between aircraft stations.

Aeronautical Station: A land station in the aeronautical mobile service. In certain instances, an aeronautical station may be placed on board a ship or an earth satellite.

Aircraft Station: A mobile station in the aeronautical mobile service on board an aircraft.

Air-Ground Communications: Two-way communication between aircraft and stations or locations on the surface of the earth.

Air Traffic: All aircraft in flight or operating on the manoeuvring area of an aerodrome.

Air Traffic Services: A generic term meaning variously, flight information service, alerting service, air traffic advisory service, air traffic control service, area control service, approach control service or aerodrome control service.

Altitude: The vertical distance of a level, a point or an object considered as a point, measured from mean sea level.

Area Control Service: A unit established to provide air traffic control service to controlled flights in control areas under its jurisdiction.

Automatic Terminal Information Service: The provision of current, routine information to arriving and departing aircraft by means of continuous and repetitive broadcasts throughout the day or a specified portion of the day.

Blind Transmission: A transmission from one station to another station in circumstances where two-way communication cannot be established but where it is believed that the called station is able to receive the transmission.

Broadcast: A transmission of information relating to air navigation that is not addressed to a specific station or stations.

Clearance Limit: The point to which an aircraft is granted an air traffic control clearance.

Expected Approach Time: The time at which ATC expects that an arriving aircraft, following a delay, will leave the holding point to complete its approach for a landing.

Flight Level: A surface of constant atmospheric pressure, which is related to a specific pressure datum, 1013.2mb, and is separated from other such surfaces by specific pressure intervals.

Flight Plan: Specified information provided to air traffic services units, relative to an intended flight or portion of a flight of an aircraft.

Heading: The direction in which the longitudinal axis of an aircraft is pointed, usually expressed in degrees from North (true, magnetic, compass or grid).

Height: The vertical distance of a level, a point, or an object considered as a point measured from a specified datum.

IFR Flight: A flight conducted in accordance with the instrument flight rules.

Instrument Meteorological Conditions: Meteorological conditions expressed in terms of visibility, horizontal and vertical distance from cloud less than the minima specified for visual meteorological conditions.

Level: A generic term relating to the vertical position of an aircraft in flight and meaning variously, height, altitude or flight level.

Missed Approach Procedure: The procedure to be followed if, after an approach, a landing is not effected.

Diagram 16

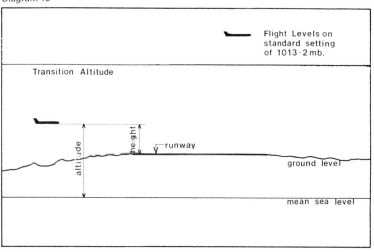

Flight Levels on standard setting of 1013·2 mb.

Transition Altitude

runway

ground level

mean sea level

Above:

Diagram illustrating the distinction between Altitude, Height and Flight Level, each of which has a precise meaning in ATC.

Diagram 17

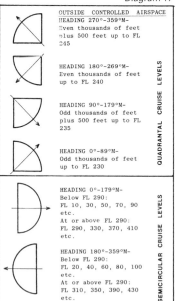

OUTSIDE CONTROLLED AIRSPACE

HEADING 270°-359°M—
Even thousands of feet plus 500 feet up to FL 245

HEADING 180°-269°M—
Even thousands of feet up to FL 240

HEADING 90°-179°M—
Odd thousands of feet plus 500 feet up to FL 235

HEADING 0°-89°M—
Odd thousands of feet up to FL 230

QUADRANTAL CRUISE LEVELS

HEADING 0°-179°M—
Below FL 290:
FL 10, 30, 50, 70, 90 etc.
At or above FL 290:
FL 290, 330, 370, 410 etc.

HEADING 180°-359°M—
Below FL 290:
FL 20, 40, 60, 80, 100 etc.
At or above FL 290:
FL 310, 350, 390, 430 etc.

SEMICIRCULAR CRUISE LEVELS

Below left:

Quadrantal rules and ICAO semicircular cruising levels.

Above right:

The various terms used in RT phraseology concerning changes in level are illustrated in this diagram.

Radar Vectoring: Provision of navigational guidance to aircraft in the form of specific headings, based on the use of radar.

Reporting Point: A specified geographical location at which the position of an aircraft is reported.

Runway Visual Range: The range over which the pilot of an aircraft on the centre line of a runway can see the runway surface markings or the lights delineating the runway or identifying its centre line.

VFR Flight: A flight conducted in accordance with the visual flight rules.

Visual Meteorological Conditions: Meteorological conditions expressed in terms of visibility, distance from cloud, and ceiling, equal to or better than specified minima.

Diagram 18

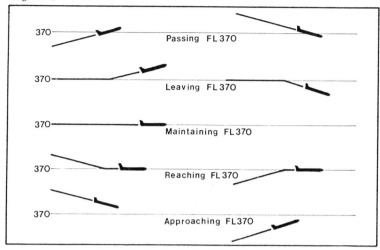

Passing FL 370

Leaving FL 370

Maintaining FL 370

Reaching FL 370

Approaching FL 370

Certain words and phrases are standard RT language, and they have the meanings given below:

Acknowledge — Let me know that you have received and understood this message.

Affirm — Yes.

Approved — Permission for proposed action granted.

Break — Indicates the separation between messages.

Cancel — Annul the previously transmitted clearance.

Check — Examine a system or procedure (no answer is normally expected).

Cleared — Authorised to proceed under the conditions specified.

Confirm — Have I correctly received the following . . .? or Did you correctly receive this message?

Contact — Establish radio contact with . . .

Correct — That is correct.

Correction — An error has been made in this transmission (or message indicated). The correct version is . . .

Disregard — Consider that transmission as not sent.

How do you read — What is the readability of my transmission.

I say again — I repeat for clarity or emphasis.

Monitor — Listen out on (frequency).

Negative — No or Permission not granted or That is not correct.

Over — My transmission is ended and I expect a response from you.

Out — This exchange of transmissions is ended and no response is expected.

Pass your message — Proceed with your message.

Read back — Repeat all, or the specified part, of this message back to me exactly as received.

Report — Pass requested information.

Request — I should like to know . . . or I wish to obtain . . .

Roger — I have received all your last transmission. *Note: Under no circumstances to be used in reply to a question requiring a direct answer in the affirmative* (Affirm) *or negative* (Negative).

Say Again — Repeat all, or the following part of your last transmission.

Speak Slower — Reduce your rate of speech.

Standby — Wait and I will call you. *Note: No onward clearance to be assumed.*

Verify — Check and confirm.

Wilco — I understand your message and will comply with it (abbreviation for will comply).

A number of other words and phrases can be heard as part of ATC transmissions, some of which are not recognised as standard radiotelephony phraseology. They are included here simply because they may be heard and not understood.

Build-up — Storm Clouds.

Charlie — Correct.

Charlie Bravo — Cumulo Nimbus (Storm) Clouds.

Expedite — Increase rate of climb or descent to a higher than normal rate.

Freecall — Change to a frequency where the transfer has not been co-ordinated (usually only used outside controlled airspace — for example for flights routeing between control zones and requiring a flight information service).

Fox Echo — QFE.

Heavy — Wide bodied aircraft leaving a turbulent wake.

Out of — Leaving (a flight level).

Pilots discretion — When ready (eg: to commence a descent).

Repeat — Say again.

Switch — Change frequency.

Uniform Frequency — UHF.

Vacating — Leaving (a flight level).

Victor Frequency — VHF.

Victor Mike — VMC.

Vortex — Wide bodied aircraft leaving a turbulent wake.

Messages transmitted by aircraft should refer at the start of the broadcast to the designation of the service being called. The main control centres for the UK are London and Scottish, and messages for these centres are prefixed London Airways (or London Control) and Scottish Airways (or Scottish Control) respectively. In practice it is usual for the full title to be used only on first contact, after which they are commonly referred to as 'London' and 'Scottish'.

Aerodrome approach control messages are prefixed with the name of the aerodrome concerned. For example, 'Heathrow Approach', 'Newcastle Approach', etc.

Similarly, transmissions for control towers also indicate the aerodrome concerned, eg 'Heathrow Tower', 'Newcastle Tower'.

Area surveillance radar messages give the name of the station providing the service, eg 'Border Radar', 'Cotswold Radar'.

Information service messages are preceded by the name of the service, eg 'London Information', 'Scottish Information'.

A study of the transcripts of actual messages given elsewhere will help to explain the procedures involved.

Aircraft Call Signs

Most scheduled aircraft which are heard on airband radios will have call signs which indicate the airline company concerned, together with its flight number. In most cases the first part will be the actual name of the airline.

However, there are a few which do not comply with this general rule, the most common of which is 'Speedbird', the call sign for most British Airways flights. A list of the majority of commercial passenger and/or freight airlines which can be heard in Britain is given in Chapter 12, together with their call signs where these differ from the name of the company.

Following the first part of the call sign there will usually be a two, three or four digit number. The majority of such call signs will have been in use for a considerable time, sometimes for several years, and some regular scheduled flights, with the same flight number, can be heard day after day, year after year. It is also common practice for outbound and inbound flights to have consecutive flight numbers. British Airways flight 179, for example, leaves London for New York every evening, and the return flight is numbered 178.

Other types of call signs are mainly numerical, for example N456789. After using the full call sign on making first contact the flight may then use an abbreviated call sign with the last three digits, eg 'November 789'.

Aircraft without flight numbers are referred to by the aircraft registration which is quoted in full on first contact. For example, G-ABCD, on initial contact would be 'Golf Alpha Bravo Charlie Delta'. After contact has been established, and provided there is no risk of confusion with other aircraft, subsequent call signs may be abbreviated to 'Golf Charlie Delta' or simply 'Charlie Delta'.

Britannia Airways, the independent British company, conveniently use the same flight number for both outbound and inbound flights except that outbound flights are followed by 'A', and inbound flights by 'B'. It is therefore possible to determine the flight direction by hearing either 'alfa' or 'bravo' as part of the call sign, but at the time of writing Britannia is the only major airline with this system.

In the case of British Airways Shuttle Services, the ATC call signs do not correspond with the flight numbers given in the timetable. The call signs currently in use are as follows:

Call sign 'Shuttle 2' —
London to Manchester
Call sign 'Shuttle 3' —
Manchester to London
Call sign 'Shuttle 4' — London to Belfast
Call sign 'Shuttle 5' — Belfast to London
Call sign 'Shuttle 6' — London to Glasgow
Call sign 'Shuttle 7' — Glasgow to London
Call sign 'Shuttle 8' —
London to Edinburgh
Call sign 'Shuttle 9' —
Edinburgh to London

In each case the flight number above is followed by a letter designation (eg 'Shuttle 2 Bravo') which varies through the day.

The first call, when an aircraft enters UK airspace, will be to establish contact with ATC on the radio frequency given by the previous sector. The transfer of control from one air traffic centre to the next will have been pre-arranged by telephone between the controllers involved, so that the new controller will be fully aware of the flight prior to the transfer taking place.

The first call should be in the following form:

a) *station being called;*
b) *station calling;*
c) *invitation to respond.*
For example:
a) *'London Airways*
b) *Lufthansa Zero Three Seven*
c) *Over.'*

In practice pilots do not always use the term 'over' and in addition they often give some of their flight details in their first transmission. The example quoted may in practice be heard as follows:

a) *'London Airways*
b) *Lufthansa Zero Three Seven*
c) *Good Morning — Flight level one five zero en route to Dover.'*

'London Airways' will respond by acknowledging the first call and will continue by giving the flight its clearance.

(A number of examples of transmissions are given later in this chapter.) Most information given by ATC will be read back

by the aircraft to ensure correct receipt and understanding. This is of great help to amateurs listening in on airband radios since it is common not to be able to receive ground transmissions due to obstructions and the distances involved.

It is not possible, of course, to fully comprehend every message when only half can be heard, but with some experience a reasonably good understanding can be achieved.

Following establishment of contact and the passing of the necessary messages, two way communication may be continued as required without the need to wait for acknowledgement of each call, although messages may be very much abbreviated.

As the aircraft approaches the edge of the particular sector, ATC will notify the flight to change frequency to the next specifying the service controller by name, eg 'Contact London on one three four decimal seven five'. Similar messages will be transmitted when the next frequency concerns another centre (eg France, Scottish, Shannon, Shanwick, Maastricht, etc) or airport (eg Heathrow Approach, Manchester, Birmingham, etc) or a radar advisory service (eg Border Radar). In each case the name of the centre will be given, eg *'Contact France on one two nine decimal zero'.*

Understanding ATC Broadcasts

Anyone listening for the first time to an ATC transmission will probably be impressed by the rapidity and abruptness of the phrases used. No time is wasted on irrelevant talk. The impression will be one of urgency, a desire to pass on information in the shortest time possible so that the next transmission may follow.

Although at first it may not appear to be the case ATC messages follow a logical and carefully organised structure, laid down in training, with an almost automatic response to situations, which ensures that the sequence of phrases is reliable and consistent. In this section the terms used, and the interpretation of the messages heard every day in the airways systems, are explained and defined. Firstly, the basic rules governing the application of ATC phraseology need to be given. ATC language covers an unusual combination of measurement systems, some imperial and some metric, which can be seen by comparing the following:

Distances are measured in nautical miles;
Speed is measured in knots;
Relative Speeds (at high level) are measured in Mach numbers;
Height is measured in feet;
Barometric pressure is measured in millibars;
Direction is measured in degrees;
Temperature is measured in degrees celsius;
Visibility is measured in kilometres or metres.

Distances
All distances shown on radio navigation charts, usually related to radio beacons, are referred to in nautical miles. One nautical mile is equal to 6,080ft compared with 5,280ft to a statute mile. The following table may be used to convert nautical miles into statute miles or kilometres:

Multiply Nautical Miles by 1.85 to obtain Kilometres
Multiply Nautical Miles by 1.15 to obtain Statute Miles
Multiply Statute Miles by 1.60 to obtain Kilometres
Multiply Statute Miles by 0.87 to obtain Nautical Miles
Multiply Kilometres by 0.54 to obtain Nautical Miles
Multiply Kilometres by 0.62 to obtain Statute Miles

For example, suppose a Radio Navigation Chart indicates the distance between two radio beacons as 69 Nautical Miles, then 69×1.15 equals 79 Statute Miles, and 69×1.85 equals 128 kilometres.

Distance Measuring Equipment (DME) carried on board aircraft, receives radio transmissions from ground beacons and enables the distance to or from that particular point to be calculated automatically.

Aircraft are therefore able to obtain precise positioning from any beacon within range with this equipment. Messages from ATC often contain references to mileages from reporting points, mainly when restrictions are placed on

requirements of ATC. A number of airways intersections, and reporting points, are identified by their relative distances to other land based navigational beacons.

DME enables aircraft to be precisely positioned, therefore ATC often refer to DME to give restrictions where these are required. As an example, '25 DME before Brookmans Park' means that the particular ATC instruction is qualified by the requirement that it applies '25 nautical miles before reaching the Brookmans Park VOR, measured on the Distance Measuring Equipment'.

Similarly, 'descend to flight level one one zero to be level thirty five miles DME from London' is translated into 'descend to flight level 110 to be at that level 35 miles before reaching the VOR at London'.

Speed
Speed of aircraft is measured in knots (nautical miles per hour). In order to compare aircraft speeds, the Mach number technique is used.

This means that speed is quoted as a ratio of the speed of sound, known as Mach number, after the Austrian physicist Ernest Mach (1838-1916). Thus Concorde cruises at Mach 2, twice the speed of sound, while conventional subsonic jet aircraft cruise at speeds around Mach 0.8. Cruising speeds are important in flight planning for controllers and the Mach number technique provides a reliable and effective means of ensuring separation. More information concerning Mach numbers is given in Chapter 7.

ATC may require aircraft to comply with certain conditions concerning aircraft speed, either in maintaining a particular speed or by reducing speed to a certain level. Approaches to airports usually specify maximum speeds, and similarly departures must comply with speed restrictions unless advised by ATC to 'cancel speed restriction'.

Height
This is one of three terms used in ATC to describe the vertical distance of an aircraft from the ground. In addition to 'height' the terms 'altitude' and 'flight level' are also used, and the three have distinct meanings in aviation and ATC.

ATC messages concerning high flying

traffic will be heard to refer to 'flight levels' as two or three digit numbers, being the level in thousands of feet with the last two digits omitted. Feet is used as the unit of measurement throughout the world, even where they are not part of the country's system of measurement. Thus flight level three seven zero indicates a flight level of 37,000ft, flight level two four zero is 24,000ft, flight level nine zero is 9,000ft and so on. However, this is much more than a simple measurement of the aircraft's vertical distance from the ground. The instrument on board the aircraft which is used to measure height is called the altimeter, which is basically a device which reacts to atmospheric pressure. As height increases, so atmospheric pressure decreases, and this change in pressure can be measured on a scale on the altimeter, calibrated to indicate hundreds and thousands of feet.

The complication which arises is that atmospheric pressure changes almost constantly, as anyone listening to the daily weather forecast will know. References to areas of 'low pressure' or 'high pressure' are well known, and as the atmospheric pressure changes in different parts of the country so the altimeter reading varies.

This means that aircraft flying at high level across either land or sea areas need to adjust their altimeters continuously to the local atmospheric pressure if they are to ensure that their height indication is correct. For high speed traffic, travelling perhaps thousands of miles every day, this would require a series of adjustments, dependent upon information provided by ground stations.

This is clearly an impractical and somewhat risky procedure, and it was soon realised that it was essential to develop a method of overcoming this difficulty. The system used worldwide is to specify a 'Standard Altimeter Setting' of 1013.2 millibars, irrespective of the actual barometric pressure. All aircraft above the specified 'Transition Altitude' (normally in the UK 3,000ft or 6,000ft) adjust their altimeters to operate on this pressure setting. All aircraft will then be operating at the same datum, with synchronised altimeters. Whether the true setting is 1013.2 millibars is irrelevant because as all aircraft are on the same setting, any error in actual height will be

common to all. The reading given by the altimeter will only be correct when the pressure is 1013.2; at all other pressures, the height will be more or less than the true height. By this means proper separation between aircraft is ensured. Any vertical distance above 'Transition Altitude' (ie when on the 1013.2 millibars setting) is termed 'Flight Level', abbreviated to FL, and spoken as thousands of feet with the last two zeros omitted, as explained earlier.

Below transition altitude, vertical distance is divided into two distinct terms, both of which rely on barometric pressures for the area in which the aircraft is operating. ATC provide aircraft with two separate barometric pressure settings, known by the abbreviations QFE and QNH. (These are sometimes referred to as 'Fox Echo' and 'November Hotel' respectively). QFE is the local atmospheric pressure setting, which, when set on the aircraft's altimeter, means that the altimeter will read zero when the aircraft is on the ground. When this setting is in use, the term used to refer to vertical distance is 'Height'.

QNH is also the local atmospheric pressure setting, but means that when this setting is set on the altimeter, the reading will be in feet above sea level. This is important for ensuring that aircraft maintain a safe clearance above ground obstructions, hills, mountains and so on. The term used to describe this vertical distance is 'Altitude'. One millibar represents approximately 30ft in height, therefore the difference in millibars between the QFE setting and the QNH setting, multiplied by 30 will give the airfield elevation above mean sea level. For example, if the QFE is given as 997 millibars and the QNH is given as 1012 millibars, the difference (15) multiplied by 30 gives the airfield elevation of approximately 450ft. The difference between QFE and QNH will always be the same for each airport.

The United Kingdom is divided into 19 regions, known as ASR's (Altimeter Setting Regions) each with a name, shown in diagram 6.

As aircraft below transition altitude pass from one ASR to another, the altimeter scale is reset to ensure the altitude is correct for the atmospheric pressure in that area. ATC may often be heard to refer to such regions when speaking to low flying aircraft (eg 'the Barnsley QNH is 998').

Another term sometimes heard to describe the local area pressure setting is 'regional'. For example 'We are at two thousand feet on the "regional" of 998'.

To summarise:

Flight Level is when aircraft are on the standard altimeter setting above Transition Altitude.

Altitude is distance above sea level.

Height is distance above the airfield.

'QNH' and 'QFE' are examples of the 'Q' code, which orginated when radio messages were transmitted in Morse, and a number of terms were simplified by using three codes starting with the letter 'Q'.

Other examples, often heard in ATC transmissions, are:

'QDM' the magnetic heading required to reach a particular station, usually an airfield, with no wind.

'QDR' the magnetic heading required to track away from a particular station. The reciprocal of QDM.

'QTE' True bearing from a particular station to an aircraft.

'QSY' Change radio frequency.

Direction

The direction in which an aircraft is flying is known as its 'heading' and is quoted in terms of degrees of the compass.

An aircraft flying due east will be on a heading of 90°, due south is 180°, due west is 270° and due north is 360° (often referred to as 'North').

Charts indicate the heading (or bearing) to be followed between navigation beacons in degrees. Aircraft flying between such points would normally be on the heading shown on the chart, except when required by ATC to alter course.

When a flight is required by ATC to remain on a particular heading it is then said to be on a 'radar heading', and this must be maintained until ATC advises either a new heading or a return to the original track.

When a flight is not on a 'radar heading' (ie one imposed by ATC) it is said to be on 'own navigation'. Messages concerning headings are often heard, especially during busy periods. Flights may be required to change direction by a speci-

fied amount, eg 'Turn left ten degrees', to stay on a particular heading, eg 'Continue the present heading until advised' or to turn on to a specified heading, eg 'Make the heading two eight zero degrees'. Other typical messages include 'Turn left ten degrees and report the new heading' and 'Turn left further ten degrees'.

When handing over the flight to the next sector controller, aircraft on a radar heading are required to inform the new sector, eg 'Change to London on one three four decimal seven five and advise the heading'.

Aircraft are often heard to refer to their direction of flight as 'steering', eg 'steering two seven zero degrees'.

The aircraft position and direction can often be deduced from ATC broadcasts related to particular headings, so from the amateur's point of view such information is invaluable.

Flight Conditions

This term refers to rules which apply to all flights, designed to ensure safe and reliable separation. There are only two sets of flight conditions:

1 Visual Flight Rules (VFR) which apply under Visual Meteorological Conditions (VMC), and

2 Instrument Flight Rules (IFR) which apply under Instrument Meteorological Conditions (IMC).

Visual Flight Rules apply to flights between 3,000ft and 25,000ft outside controlled airspace only when it is possible for the pilot to have good visibility (minimum five nautical miles) and to remain separated from cloud by one nautical mile horizontally and 1,000ft vertically.

At or below 3,000ft AMSL in uncontrolled airspace, the pilot must be able to see the ground and be clear of cloud.

Under VFR the pilot must keep a good lookout because remaining clear of other traffic is his (or her) responsibility. Furthermore, if flying under Instrument Flight Rules in VMC, remaining clear of traffic is also the pilot's responsibility.

Airways and certain other areas of controlled airspace may not be flown in VFR conditions.

A variety of terms and abbreviations are used by aircraft and ATC when referring to flight conditions, and a few are quoted here. Visual Flight Rules are often referred to as 'VFR' or as 'Victor Fox'. Similarly Visual Meteorological Conditions may be known as 'VMC' or 'Victor Mike'. For example, an aircraft referring to the flight conditions as 'Victor Mike on top' is interpreted as meaning 'VMC conditions above cloud'.

Instrument Flight Rules come into force when the visibility conditions described in the previous section cannot be applied. The aircraft is, therefore, required to fly 'on instruments' due to the flight conditions, and only suitably qualified pilots with properly equipped aircraft may operate in such conditions. Furthermore the responsibility for separation from other aircraft now transfers to the ground controllers when flying within controlled airspace.

Aircraft flying IMC above the transition altitude must adjust their altimeters to the standard setting of 1013.2 millibars and fly in accordance with what is known as the 'quadrantal rule', which is devised to ensure that aircraft remain clear of each other by at least 500ft.

Under this rule aircraft flying on a magnetic track between 000° and 089° must fly at odd thousands of feet. In the second quarter of the circle with magnetic tracks between 90° and 179°, the flight levels must be at odd thousands of feet *plus 500ft.*

In the third quarter, between 180° and 269°, flight levels are in even thousands of feet.

Finally, in the fourth quarter, between 270° and 359° flight levels must be in even thousands of feet *plus 500ft.*

The quadrantal cruising levels only apply in the UK FIR below flight level 245, outside controlled airspace.

Within controlled airspace, ICAO semi-circular standard cruising levels apply. Below flight level 290, aircraft heading in an easterly direction (between 0° and 179°) fly at levels 10, 30, 50, 70, 90, etc up to 290. At and above 290, the flight levels are 290, 330, 370, 410, etc in multiples of 4,000ft. Aircraft heading in a westerly direction (180° to 359°) fly at levels 20, 40, 60, 80, 100 up to 280. Above 280, flight levels are 310, 350, 390, 430, etc in multiples of 4,000ft.

Quadrantal cruising levels and ICAO standard semicircular cruising levels are shown in diagram 17.

Special Visual Flight Rules (VFR) Flights

A Special VFR flight is one which is given clearance to operate in a Control Zone or in Special Rules Airspace even though it is unable to comply with Instrument Flight Rules. The pilot must remain clear of cloud and have the surface in sight at all times, and all ATC instructions must be followed. Requests for a Special VFR flight must be made with a least 10 minutes' notice, either by telephone to the appropriate ATC unit or by radio when the aircraft is in flight. A flight plan is not required but full details are required, including the estimated time of arrival at the point of entry into controlled airspace.

Time

In air traffic control transmissions, time may be referred to as 'local' or as Greenwich Mean Time (GMT). Another term used to indicate GMT is 'Zulu'.

'Local' time is, of course, the time applicable to the area being referred to.

In aviation, particularly where long range journeys are concerned, there is usually no need to refer to hours, and time is usually expressed only in minutes, unless there is likely to be confusion.

Transmissions will, therefore, be heard to refer to minutes only, mainly in connection with estimated times for reaching reporting points or for arrivals at destinations.

As an example, 'Speedbird five one three one just passed Fawley, Midhurst at three three' indicates that the flight estimates reaching the Midhurst beacon at 33 minutes past the hour.

Weather

Chapter 9 deals with weather conditions and an explanation of the terms involved, so mention is made here of only a few commonly heard expressions in ATC transmissions.

Poor visibility is always a problem for arriving aircraft, and when conditions are poor aircraft will require frequent updates on local conditions in order that a decision on possible diversions can be made.

The main term to be heard is the Runway Visual Range (RVR) which is given in metres for each runway. Runway Visual Range (RVR) is usually given as three separate readings — one at the runway threshold, the second at the midpoint position, and the third at the stop end — the end of the runway.

A second common term to be heard concerns cumulonimbus storm clouds (CB) which can result in severe buffeting of the aircraft. Pilots will always do their best to avoid such clouds, and they can often be heard asking for permission to change course accordingly. Some examples are:

'May we turn left ten to avoid weather?'
'May we turn left ten to avoid CB?'
'May we turn to the left to avoid Charlie Bravo?'
'May we go to the right twenty degrees to go round a build-up?'

All such transmissions concern stormy weather conditions and when such conditions prevail across the country many aircraft change course almost constantly as they zigzag along the airway. In each of the examples quoted above, the aircraft is requesting permission to change direction to avoid bad weather.

The Inertial Navigation System
This is the modern aircraft navigational computer used on all long range aircraft. However, as it is often referred to by aircraft it is also mentioned briefly here.

The Inertial Navigation System allows an aircraft to navigate precisely without reference to radio beacons, and pilots often request direct routeings if they are so equipped.

Aircraft may be heard making reference to INS, asking ATC for direct routeings, including in their message the fact that they are 'INS equipped'.

Messages from ATC which relate to clearances involving the inertial navigation system can be heard frequently, particularly during relatively quiet periods.

A typical message might be *'Route INS direct to Pole Hill',* indicating that the aircraft is cleared to route outside airways and without the aid of navigation radio beacons.

Changes in height
This gives rise to a number of descriptive terms, each with a precise meaning. It is obviously important that such terms are not interchanged otherwise confusion and misinterpretation could result.

The most common phrases to be heard in transmissions are explained in the following examples.

Aircraft increasing height use the term 'climb', eg *'TWA seven five three climb flight level two eight zero'.* Reducing height is indicated by the term 'descend', eg *'Cyprus two three seven descend flight level one two zero'.*

Note that in these first two examples 'climb' and 'descend' are used, rather than 'ascend' and 'descend' since these latter words, with their similar sounds, could easily be misunderstood, particularly in conditions of poor reception or where pilots who are not English speaking are involved.

Aircraft remaining at one particular level are said to be 'maintaining' the flight level.

Aircraft which are descending, or climbing, use the term 'passing' to describe the actual flight level through which the aircraft is passing at the time the message is transmitted, eg *'Speedbird two five six passing three three zero for two five zero'* means that BA 256 is descending through 33,000ft for 25,000ft, the flight level to which it has been cleared.

Aircraft which have been given clearance to climb (or descend) will notify ATC when they commence the climb (or the descent) by the term 'leaving'. For example, a clearance to climb from 8,000ft to 12,000ft would be acknowledged as *'Shamrock one five nine leaving flight level eight zero for flight level one two zero'* as it commences the climb.

Aircraft arriving at a particular flight level may use the term 'reaching' (eg *'Reaching flight level three seven zero'*).

References to other aircraft are often heard in ATC transmissions advising a particular flight of other traffic in the area. It is common practice to use a conventional 'clock' system as a means of reference, in preference to compass bearings. An example illustrating a typical transmission is shown in diagram 19.

In the example shown, a British Airways 737 flight BA 454 is on a heading of 180°. A second British Airways flight, BA266 is on a heading of 100°. As the 737 is cutting across the path of the other aircraft, a typical ATC transmission would read something like:

'Speedbird two six six, you may see company traffic in your eleven o'clock, range twelve miles passing left to right, flight level one eight zero. It's a seven three seven'.

AC: *'Roger Speedbird two six six, we have the traffic'.*

Diagram 19

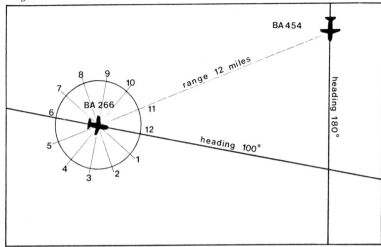

It can be seen from the illustration that from BA 266, assuming that straight ahead is 12 o'clock, the position of the other aircraft is roughly at 11 o'clock, thus the pilot is given a clear guide that he should look slightly to the left of dead ahead.

The inclusion of the word 'company' in the message indicates that the other aircraft is owned by the same company, ie both flights are British Airways.

(Contrary to popular belief, aircraft in flight do not use radar to obtain warning of other traffic, but instead must rely on ground controllers to advise them of conflicting flights. Visual contact can obviously only occur in suitable weather conditions.)

Occasionally, in conditions of poor reception ATC may ask another aircraft on the same frequency which is within range, to 'relay' a message to the first aircraft.

Invariably this is successful simply because the relaying aircraft has the advantage of height and usually has no difficulty in making contact.

Secondary Surveillance Radar

Conventional (or primary) radar depends for its efficient operation on the reflection from a 'target' — for example, an aircraft — which is received by the radar antenna and displayed on the controller's radar screen as a point of bright light. The range of primary radar is limited by the strength of

Example of the 'clock' reference system. Details are given in the text.

the signal from the ground based transmitter which is reflected back to the ground receiver by the aircraft, and also by the aircraft's height above the horizon.

Secondary surveillance radar, however, differs from primary radar in that the signal transmitted by the ground station is received by the aircraft via a piece of equipment on the flightdeck — the transponder — which then re-transmits the signal back to the ground station. The power required to produce a return signal is therefore far less with secondary radar than with primary radar, which depends only on a reflected signal. The range of SSR is up to twice that available with primary radar.

In addition, whilst primary radar displays the position of the aircraft target, secondary radar is capable of questioning the various systems on the flight deck and having those details transmitted back to a computer at the Air Traffic Control Centre.

Before the flight departs on its journey a flight plan will have been filed giving detailed information on the routeing, aircraft type, callsign, etc and these facts will be fed into the computer, together with a four figure identification number which

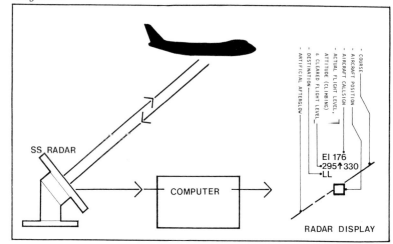

Diagram 20

COMPUTER

SS RADAR

RADAR DISPLAY

EI 176
295 ↑ 330
LL

- COURSE
- AIRCRAFT POSITION
- AIRCRAFT CALLSIGN
- ACTUAL FLIGHT LEVEL,
  ATTITUDE (CLIMBING)
  & CLEARED FLIGHT LEVEL
- DESTINATION
- ARTIFICIAL AFTERGLOW

Secondary surveillance radar interrogates the transponder on the flight deck and the 'reply' shows the aircraft position and flight details on the controller's radar screen.

will be exclusive to that flight in UK airspace on that particular day. Many airlines provide scheduled service details weeks or months in advance and the information is stored in the system until the day of the flight. The four figure code number is known as the 'squawk', and this word is part of the everday language of air traffic control messages.

A flight in controlled airspace, having been allocated a particular squawk number as part of the ATC clearance, will be required to select the appropriate code on the aircraft's transponder. A selective signal from the ground radar station will be transmitted to the aircraft, whereupon the transponder will process the signal and return the message to the ground, including the four figure squawk code.

The information is routed through the ATC computer, the squawk code being related to the particular flight plan. Included with the message are details of the flight level and the 'attitude' of the aircraft (ie: climbing or descending). When the computer has sorted the data the radar signal is then passed to the radar controller's screen, which displays the aircraft position, its passing level, an arrow indicating whether the aircraft is in the climb or the descent, and the cleared flight level. The destination may also be shown. The process in fact takes less time than it does to read about it! When first contacting the UK control centre, the flight is usually requested to squawk 'ident', which means that the flight crew operate an identity button which causes the particular radar return to increase in intensity or to visually stand out in some other way.

Squawk codes can be used for several other situations to provide ATC with invaluable information on the progress of the flight. Code 7700, for example, is the code used to denote an emergency on-board condition. Code 7600 indicates radio failure, while code 7500 warns the controller of some unlawful interference with the flight. The squawk of 4321 is used by aircraft — usually General Aviation flights — which are operating outside controlled airspace. Aircraft with radio problems may be asked by ATC to squawk ident if the transmissions are being received, thus indicating to the ground that radio reception is functioning.

A further development in the use of secondary surveillance radar is the ability of transponders to not only pass information to the ground, but to question transponders fitted to other aircraft in the vicinity, thereby obtaining independently

44

the details of those flights which might be on a potentially conflicting course.

The system, Traffic Collision and Avoidance System (TCAS) is currently on test in the USA.

In the future, the provision of 'Mode S' SSR transponders to aircraft will enable ten times the information to be passed between the flight and the ground. The various systems in the aircraft are linked to the transponder so that many aspects of the flight details (eg: speed, heading, level etc) can be continuously and automatically passed to the ground. Weather information can also be obtained on a continuous basis from every aircraft fitted with Mode S.

Control information may be provided on request to pilots via the datalink.

Mode S is to be fitted to all aircraft used for civil aviation in the 21st century.

Transmissions

The following section consists of ATC broadcasts and aircraft responses, covering a variety of different circumstances. Every message is reproduced here word by word, with numerals written out in full so that there will be no misunderstanding as to the radio telephony procedures being followed. This section does not include messages concerning oceanic clearances (see chapter 7), airport arrivals and departures (see chapter 6) or 'company' messages (see chapter 11). By reading through these messages, it should be possible to become acquainted in a fairly short time with the procedures being used in ATC today, and they will enable the complete beginner to recognise phrases and technical terms. Throughout the book a message from the ground is prefixed 'ATC', and the aircraft message is indicated as 'AC'. Most messages heard on radio can be related to one of the quoted examples, thus enabling rapid familiarisation with ATC practice. Actual messages are given in italic lettering. Position reporting is one of the principal methods used in air traffic control to ensure safe separation, in which the positions of every flight is noted by the controller, together with estimated times for other reporting points along the route.

The following items of information are to be included in the report:

— Aircraft call-sign
— Position
— Time

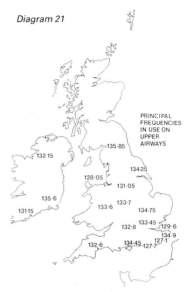

Diagram 21

PRINCIPAL FREQUENCIES IN USE ON UPPER AIRWAYS

135·85
132·15
134·25
128·05
131·05
135·6
133·7
133·6
131·15
134·75
132·8   133·45
129·6
134·9
132·6   134·45–127·5   127·1

UK map indicating the principal VHF frequencies for high altitude controlled airspace.

— Level
— Next position
— Estimated time of Arrival

For example:

— IBERIA 226
— ORTAC
— 26
— Flight Level 310
— SOUTHAMPTON
— 35

The actual transmission would read as follows:
London good morning, IBERIA two two Six, passing ORTAC at two six, flight level three one zero estimating SOUTHAMPTON at three five, requesting descent.

The controller might then reply:
IBERIA two two six London good morning to you, maintain flight level three one zero, standard routeing SOUTHAMPTON, MIDHURST, OCKHAM for London Heathrow landing runway two eight right, squawk five four seven six. Descent clearance in ten miles.

Diagram 22

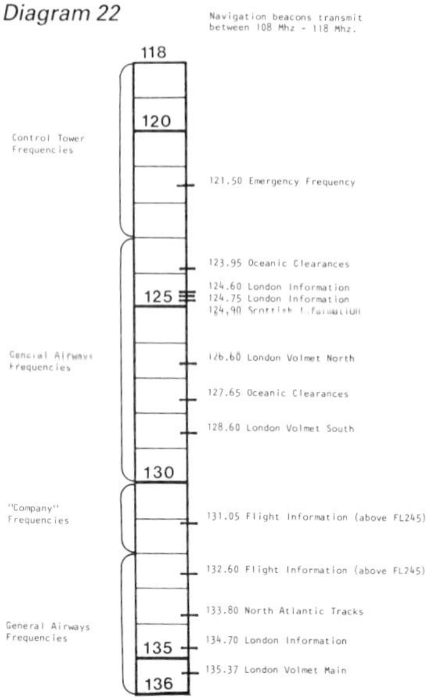

Navigation beacons transmit
between 108 Mhz - 118 Mhz.

118

120

Control Tower
Frequencies

121.50 Emergency Frequency

123.95 Oceanic Clearances

124.60 London Information
125 ≡ 124.75 London Information
124.90 Scottish Information

General Airways
Frequencies

126.60 London Volmet North

127.65 Oceanic Clearances

128.60 London Volmet South

130

"Company"
Frequencies

131.05 Flight Information (above FL245)

132.60 Flight Information (above FL245)

133.80 North Atlantic Tracks

General Airways
Frequencies

134.70 London Information

135

135.37 London Volmet Main

136

Guide to VHF airband frequencies in the range 118MHz to 136 MHz.

Note that the initial contact between aircraft and ground control first specifies the station being called (London) followed by the station calling (IBERIA two two six).

Pilots are expected to read back in full certain ATC instructions, as follows:

Level instructions
Heading instructions
Speed instructions
Airways or route clearances
Runway clearances
Secondary Surveillance Radar instructions
Altimeter Settings
VDF information
Frequency changes

MESSAGES

AC: *London Control, this is the Clipper one hundred at eight west, level three seven zero estimate Lands End at five three, Southampton next.*

ATC: *Clipper one zero zero Roger good evening, maintain flight level three seven zero, standard route Lands End, Southampton, Ockham for London Heathrow, landing runway two eight right. Squawk ident on five four seven zero.*

AC: *Roger ident five four seven zero standard route for Heathrow, two eight right Clipper one hundred.*

(Pan American Flight 100 reports to London Control at 50° North 8° West at flight level 370. The next reporting point is at LANDS END with SOUTHAMPTON reporting point next.
The flight is cleared by London on the standard arrival route (STAR) to Heathrow, where the runway in use is 28R. Clipper 100 is instructed to identify itself by 'squawking' code 5470.)

ATC: *Lufthansa four five one London what is your Mach number?*

AC: *Lufthansa four five one Mach decimal eight two.*

ATC: *Roger — break — Sabena two two six what is your Mach number?*

AC: *Eight one two two six.*

ATC: *Roger.*

ATC: *Lufthansa four five one speed not less than decimal eight two*

AC: *Roger not less than eight two Lufthansa four five one.*

ATC: *Sabena two two six London, speed not greater than decimal eight one.*

AC: *Speed not greater than decimal eight one Sabena two two six. We have the other aircraft in sight at one o'clock.*

ATC: *Sabena two two six understood.*

(Two aircraft are on the same route, Lufthansa 451 being ahead of Sabena 226. To maintain separation, London Control instructs minimum and maximum speeds to the two aircraft in terms of Mach numbers.)

AC: *Dan Air three seven two passing flight level two seven zero for two nine zero — may we continue to three three zero?*

ATC: *Dan Air three seven two negative maintain flight level two nine zero on reaching — there is crossing traffic at three three zero, left to right, on Upper Red one. Expect further climb in fifteen miles.*

AC: *Roger understood Dan Air three seven two — looking.*

Diagram 23

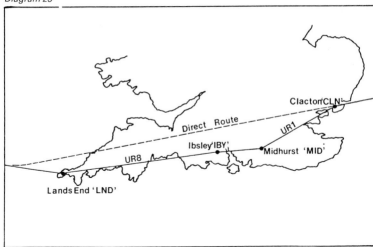

AC: *Dan Air three seven two traffic in sight.*

ATC: *Roger three seven two.*

(Later)

ATC: *Dan Air three seven two London, well clear of the traffic now, continue climb to flight level three three zero.*

AC: *Climb flight level three three zero Dan Air three seven two thank you. Out of two nine zero now.*

(Dan Air 372 is prevented from climbing to FL 330 due to conflicting 'traffic' — ie: another aircraft — at FL 330 ahead, crossing from the left towards the right. After the other aircraft has moved away, Dan Air 372 is cleared to climb.)

AC: *Speedbird five four four two good morning out of flight level nine zero for one three zero, heading three six zero.*

ATC: *Speedbird five four four two good morning continue climb to flight level two six zero.*

AC: *Continue climb to flight level two six zero, five four four two.*

ATC: *Five four four two are you avoiding weather?*

AC: *Negative five four four two.*

ATC: *Roger, turn left onto a radar heading of three five zero.*

High level flights are often given direct routeings which take them well away from the normal upper airways. The flight remains under positive ATC control.

Civil Aviation Authority

AC: *Three five zero radar heading five four four two.*

(Speedbird 5442 is routeing northwards from London Heathrow and is given climb to FL 260. The controller asks whether the pilot is 'avoiding weather' — in other words avoiding cumulo nimbus storm clouds. The controller then directs the pilot to turn left 10°.)

AC: *Britannia one nine zero Bravo London good evening flight level three five zero, four two DME from Berry Head, for Glasgow.*

ATC: *London Britannia one nine zero Bravo good evening, maintain flight level three five zero, Upper Amber twenty five, standard for Glasgow, squawk ident on three four two two.*

AC: *Ident on three four two two, standard for Glasgow, maintain flight level three five zero, Britannia one nine zero Bravo. Any chance of Berry Head direct to the GOW — we are INS equipped.*

ATC: *Britannia one nine zero Bravo stand by.*

ATC: *Britannia one nine zero Bravo route from your present position direct to the Golf Oscar Whisky.*

AC: *Direct to the GOW one nine zero Bravo thanks very much.*

(Britannia 190B checks in with London 42 miles before reaching Berry Head beacon, and is cleared on Upper Amber 25 to Glasgow. A direct route to the Glasgow beacon — Golf Oscar Whisky or GOW — is requested by the pilot. 'INS' is the type of navigation equipment on the aircraft which is independent of the navigation beacon system. [INS is Inertial Navigation System].)

AC: *London Control TWA eight eight one good day approaching Lizard flight level three nine zero.*

ATC: *Transworld eight eight one good morning maintain flight level three nine zero route Upper Green four fifty north eight west for Kennedy. Do you have your Oceanic clearance?*

AC: *Affirmative TWA eight eight one its track Charlie at three nine zero.*

ATC: *Roger eight eight one confirm that you expect to enter the Oceanic area not before time two five?*

AC: *Affirmative eight eight one. Understand fifty north and eight west not before two five — we are reducing speed to lose time.*

ATC: *That's understood TWA eight eight one.*

(TWA881 is en route to Kennedy airport in the USA, and expects to enter the Shanwick Oceanic Area at 50° North and 08° West at 25 minutes past the hour. The time limit has been imposed by Shanwick and in order to comply TWA 881 must reduce speed for a short while. Alternatively, aircraft are occasionally required to orbit — ie: fly in a circle — to lose time.)

ATC: *Britannia two two five Alfa there is a seven four seven at your flight level crossing left to right about thirty miles ahead — caution turbulent wake.*

AC: *OK Sir we can see the traffic — thanks for the warning.*

ATC advises Britannia 225A to beware of the turbulence created by a Boeing 747 at the same level.

AC: *Dan Air four five one could you ask the French if we can route direct to Santiago?*

ATC: *Standby Dan Air four five one — we're already working on that — I'll call you back.*

AC: *Roger standing by.*

ATC: *Dan Air four five one after crossing the boundary you may route direct to Santiago — this will keep you clear of an active danger area.*

AC: *Thank you Sir after crossing the boundary direct Santiago Dan Air four five one.*

A 'direct' route is approved by ATC after co-ordination with French control.

AC: *Lufthansa four three seven London we are experiencing moderate turbulence at flight level three seven zero — have you had any previous reports?*

Diagram 24

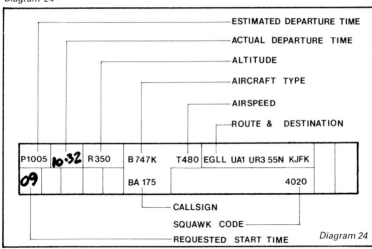

Diagram 24

Diagram 25

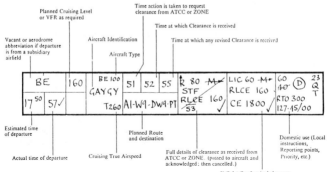

Diagram 26

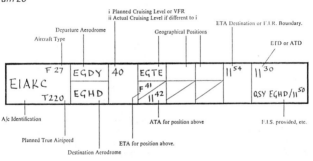

49

Diagram 27

Above......ft	+......	Co-ordination Effected	⊖	Radar vectoring for a visual approach	R/V
......ft or above	......+	Current weather	WX	Radar vectoring for ILS approach	R/I
After passing	/	Delay not determined	Z	Release not before	(time)
Aircraft given time check	T	Descend	↓	Release not before	R(time) (for use with data transfer systems)
Aircraft given appropriate altimeter setting	Q	Descent co-ordinated	₵		
Aircraft instructed to hold	H	Expected approach time	EAT		
Aircraft has reported at wrong level (indicated in circle)	e.g. ⑧⓪	Flight Priority Letter (indicated in circle)	e.g. Ⓐ	Release subject to ...... (callsign or title, aircraft or agency)	RS
Alternative instructions	(......)	ILS	I	Report leaving (level)	RL
Below......ft	−......	Joining flight	=	Report Passing (level)	RP
......ft or below	......−	Leaving controlled airspace	△	Report reaching (level)	RR
Climb	↑	Maintain	M	Request flight level change en route	RLCE
Climb co-ordinated	⇡	No delay expected	∧	Restrictions written below this line	——
Climb 1,000 ft below (aircraft)	↑(a/c callsign)	Outer Marker	OM	Reporting Point	F
Climb when instructed by radar	↑R	Overhead	QFG	Slot time	F(for use with data transfer systems)
Cruise climb	↑CC	Overflight	V	Surveillance Radar Approach	SRA
Cleared to cross airways/ADR	×			This information has been passed and acknowledged.	√
Clearance expires at (time)	CE	Radar	R		

ATC: *Negative four three seven, that's the first report I've had — do you wish to descend?*

AC: *Affirmative Lufthansa four three seven.*

ATC: *Roger Lufthansa four three seven descend now flight level three three zero.*

AC: *Cleared flight level three three zero Lufthansa four three seven — leaving three seven zero now — thank you.*

(Later)

AC: *Lufthansa four three seven levelling flight level three three zero — the turbulence has smoothed out now.*

ATC: *Roger Lufthansa four three seven.*

Flights in conditions of turbulence are usually given alternative levels as soon as they can be arranged by ATC.

Details of marking symbols for flight Progress Strips.

Right:
A Flight Information Centre showing the procedure board. Each 'Flight Strip' concerns a separate flight.
International Aeradio Ltd

5 Charts and other Publications

To the enthusiast, possession of a set of radio navigation charts is almost as important as an airband radio. Charts portray, in great detail, the various air routes and radio facilities world-wide, and all are readily available to the general public at surprisingly low prices.

En-route charts showing the airways are obtainable in the UK from three sources, detailed later, and their respective addresses are given in Chapter 12.

Although the charts produced by the three organisations show basically identical information, there are differences in the colouring systems and in the details of some facilities. Also, there are sometimes variations in the areas covered. For example, only the RAF charts for the UK show the whole of the British Isles on one sheet. It is highly recommended that, if possible, a copy of each of the available publications is obtained to decide on the one which suits you best. Diagrams 28, 29 and 30 show extracts from each of the three available sources, covering the same area. Black and white reproduction, however, does not do justice to the real thing and these should only be looked upon as a guide.

En-Route Charts
En-route charts are produced by three organisations for the UK:
1 Royal Air Force;
2 British Airways 'Aerad';
3 Jeppesen.

Royal Air Force
The Royal Air Force supplies an excellent range of radio navigation charts for the UK, produced on stiff paper, and covering the whole country in two publications, reference 411H for high altitude, and 412S-L and 412N-L for low altitude. A feature of these charts is that certain military routes and North Sea Oilfields are also shown. The scales to which the low level charts are drawn is roughly 14 nautical miles to the inch, while High Level charts are approximately 28nm per inch. In addition to the charts, a variety of other information is available, providing the enthusiast with a mass of invaluable data. Obtain a copy of their catalogue of Flight Information Publications (called 'FLIPS'). All publications are available by post from the address given in chapter 12.

Below:
Part of the high altitude UK chart produced by Jeppesen. Similar details are shown in diagrams 29 and 30.

Diagram 29

British Airways 'AERAD'

'Aerad' charts are probably the best known to the public, and they are available through many sales outlets in the UK. The UK charts cover high altitude (H109/108) to a scale of 30 nautical miles to the inch, covering most of Europe (except Spain and the north of Scotland) extending from Ireland to Egypt. Low altitude is covered in EUR1/2, as far north as Edinburgh, and includes parts of France and Germany. The remainder of Scotland is shown on a separate chart, EUR3. The scale is approximately 17 nautical miles to the inch.

Aerad produce a wide range of charts and similar related publications concerning ATC. Included in their range are Standard Instrument Departure Charts, Standard Arrival Charts, Noise Abatement routes for airports, plans of airports, ramp details and details of docking procedures for various aircraft types.

Jeppesen

These charts are produced by Jeppesen Sanderson Inc of America, and are available in the UK from CSE Aviation, who will provide a catalogue on request. Jeppesen covers a large selection of publications, ranging from charts and information publications to cassette tapes covering ATC procedures. Two charts cover the UK, one for high altitude (reference E(H1) 3 and 4) and one for low altitude (reference E(LO) 1 and 2). The first is to a scale of 20 nautical miles to the inch, the second is partly 20nm to the inch and partly 15nm to the inch.

Part of the high altitude UK chart produced by the Royal Air Force. Similar details are shown in diagrams 28 and 30.

Civil Aviation Authority

The Civil Aviation Authority also distributes a number of charts and other items relating to aeronautical information. They are available from Messrs Edward Stanford Ltd, International Aeradio, Airtour International, the Aircraft Owners and Pilots' Association, or direct from the Chart Room of the CAA. The addresses of each of these suppliers are given in chapter 12

CAA charts include the following:

Topographical charts, Instructional Plotting Charts, Aerodrome Obstruction Charts, Standard Departure and Standard Arrival Charts, Charts of UK restrictions, intense aerial activity and military flying, and Helicopter Routes. Part of one of the Standard Departure charts published by the CAA is shown in diagram 39.

Charts are updated on a 28-day cycle, under an agreed system known as AIRAC, — Air Information Regulation and Control. Depending on your level of enthusiasm, you may decide to update your charts perhaps once a year, or, if you can afford it, every month! Changes do occur, but fundamental revisions are rare and frequent replacement of charts is probably unjustified for amateur purposes. Even pilots of international airlines may be heard occasionally, complaining that their flight-

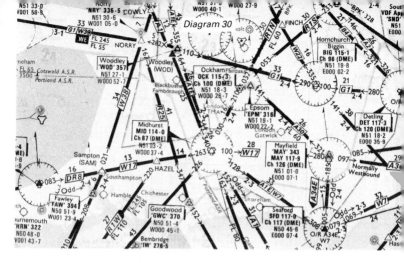

Diagram 30

Part of the high altitude UK chart produced by Aerad. Similar details are shown in diagrams 28 and 29.

deck charts are not up to date!

Oceanic charts, covering the polar areas and the North Atlantic ocean, are also available and are of particular interest when understanding the oceanic track system.

In addition, of course, en-route charts for any part of the world can be obtained from the same sources.

Understanding the Information

All airways, beacons and reporting points are shown fairly clearly, although it may take some practice before details can be taken in. The first impression on seeing a chart might probably be of a bewildering mass of lines and figures, but after studying the map the details will start to become clear.

The radio navigation beacons are identified by name and a 3-letter abbreviation. 'Dover', for example, is identified as 'DVR' and may be referred to by ATC and by aircraft as 'Dover' or 'Delta Victor Romeo'. Also shown will be the frequency on which the beacon signal is broadcast. In this example, 'Dover' transmits on 117.7MHz and by tuning in to this frequency on an airband radio, the signal 'DVR' in Morse code will be heard, provided, of course, that the beacon is within range. All VOR beacons transmit on frequencies between

108MHz and 118MHz, therefore it is very probable that one can be heard in most areas of the UK.

Compulsory reporting points (often co-inciding with VOR's) are shown as solid black triangles, located on airways, airways intersections or on boundaries between adjacent control areas. However, in spite of being designated as 'compulsory' not all flights are required to report when passing such points. ATC may sometimes be heard to direct pilots to 'omit position reports on this frequency', and in these cases aircraft may cover large distances without talking to ATC.

Reporting points which are to be used 'on request' are shown as white triangles.

Some reporting points are not given place names, but may instead be known by other titles such as 'Haddock', 'Bream', 'Bluebell' and so on, or sometimes by a pair of letters. For example, 'Echo Alpha' and 'Echo Bravo' are both reporting points in the English Channel.

Overleaf:
Jeppesen chart of Manchester International Airport showing the parking bays. The same information is shown in diagram 32 by Aerad.

Facing page:
Aerad chart of Manchester International Airport showing the parking bays. The same information is shown in diagram 31 by Jeppesen.

TAXI

Diagram 31

MANCHESTER, U.K.
MANCHESTER INTL

(10-5 A) 24 FEB 84

JEPPESEN

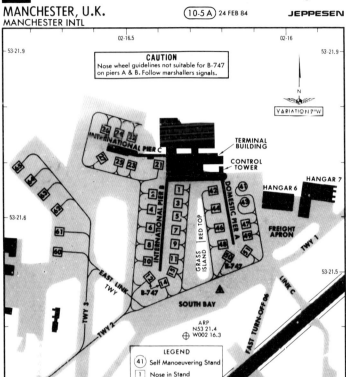

CAUTION
Nose wheel guidelines not suitable for B-747 on piers A & B. Follow marshallers signals.

TERMINAL BUILDING

CONTROL TOWER

HANGAR 6

HANGAR 7

INTERNATIONAL PIER C

INTERNATIONAL PIER B

DOMESTIC PIER A

FREIGHT APRON

RED TOP

GRASS ISLAND

EAST LINK TWY

B-747

SOUTH BAY

TWY 3

TWY 2

TWY 1

LINK C

FAST TURN-OFF 06

ARP
N53 21.4
W002 16.3

LEGEND
(41) Self Manoeuvering Stand
[1] Nose in Stand

PARKING PROCEDURES

PUSH-BACK (During work in progress on apron areas).

1. Aircraft departing from Stand Numbers 1, 3 and 5 on International Pier BRAVO and from Stand Numbers 42 and 44 on Domestic Pier ALPHA are to manoeuvre as follows: aircraft are to be pushed back to face SOUTH and then will be towed forward until abeam Stand Number 46 (on Domestic Pier Alpha) until clear of the Red Top area of the apron before taxiing under their own power.

2. Wide bodied aircraft departing from Stand Number 22 on International Pier CHARLIE are to be towed forward along the taxiway route until abeam Stand Number 26 before taxiing under their own power.

3. Operators of DC 10 and Tri-Star aircraft must not start the tail mounted engine until abeam Stand Number 26 (tug disconnect position).

NOTE: On push back, aircraft wheels are to remain clear of the red top area. Pilots are to request permission from ATC to "push-back" on nose-in-stands.

Stands 60-64: Push back to face south and exit via apron taxiway centre line.

Stand 65: Angled push back and pull forward to abeam stand 64 before applying minimum break away power.

CHANGES: Push-back procedures.

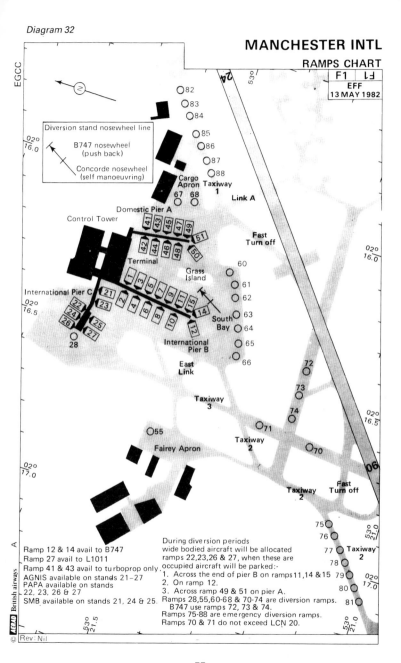

Diagram 32

MANCHESTER INTL
RAMPS CHART

F1	F1

EFF
13 MAY 1982

EGCC

Diversion stand nosewheel line

B747 nosewheel
(push back)

Concorde nosewheel
(self manoeuvring)

○82
○83
○84
○85
○86
○87
○88

Cargo Apron   Taxiway 1
67 68

Link A

Domestic Pier A

Control Tower

41 43 45 47 49
51
42 44 46 48 50

Fast Turn off

Terminal

Grass Island

60
○61
○62
○63
○64
○65
○66

International Pier C
21
22 23
24 25
26 27
28

1 3 5 7 9 11 15
2 4 6 8 10 13 14
12

South Bay

International Pier B

East Link

72
73
74
71
70

Taxiway 3

○55

Fairey Apron

Taxiway 2

Taxiway 2

Fast Turn off

75
76
77   Taxiway 2
78
79
80
81

Ramp 12 & 14 avail to B747
Ramp 27 avail to L1011
Ramp 41 & 43 avail to turboprop only.
AGNIS available on stands 21–27
PAPA available on stands
22, 23, 26 & 27
SMB available on stands 21, 24 & 25.

During diversion periods
wide bodied aircraft will be allocated
ramps 22,23,26 & 27, when these are
occupied aircraft will be parked:-
1. Across the end of pier B on ramps 11,14 & 15
2. On ramp 12.
3. Across ramp 49 & 51 on pier A.
Ramps 28,55,60-68 & 70-74 are diversion ramps.
B747 use ramps 72, 73 & 74.
Ramps 75-88 are emergency diversion ramps.
Ramps 70 & 71 do not exceed LCN 20.

British airways

© Rev: Nil

55

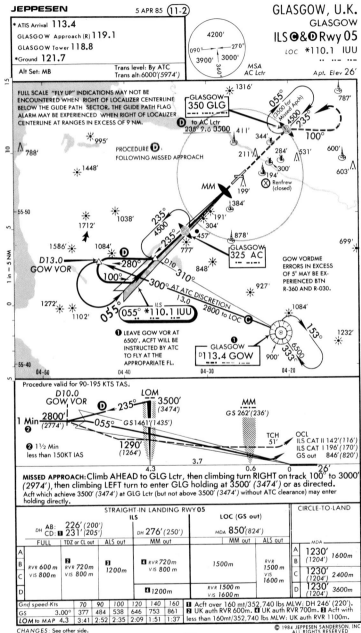

Left:
Glasgow Radar Arrival chart by Jeppesen.

Reporting points in the same area are sometimes linked by common names, eg 'Elder', 'Hazel', 'Willow', in southeast England.

In a few cases, the reporting point may be adjacent to another nearby VOR, as in the case of a reporting point on airway Amber 2 in the Midlands, known as 'Abeam Daventry'.

Pilots sometimes refer to reporting points by names which are not actually those appearing on the charts. 'Glasgow', for example, which is designated Golf Alpha Whisky, is often quoted as 'the GOW' (rhyming with 'how'). Brookmans Park is called 'The Park', and Pole Hill may be heard as either 'The Pole' or 'The Hill'. The sharp turn at Ibsley for aircraft approaching London from Ortac on Airway UR14 is referred to as 'The Bend'. Berry Head is known as 'The Head'.

Bear in mind that the name given to a beacon does not necessarily mean that it is actually located at the place stated, although it will be somewhere in the area. For example, the VOR beacon at Brecon in South Wales is actually sited just outside New Tredegar, some 20 miles to the south of Brecon town.

It is easy to plot exactly the location of the VOR beacons shown on the charts by using an Ordnance Survey map. The Landranger 1:50,000 scale is ideal. Each VOR beacon on Jeppesen and Aerad charts has the precise latitude and longitude given alongside, and by relating these two figures to the latitude and longitude given on the perimeter of the Ordnance Survey sheet the exact location can be found. As the VOR beacon is situated on the centre line of the airway, the exact position of each airway is also obtained.

Every airway is identified by a letter and a number and the bearing of the airway is given in both directions. For example, Amber 1 between Prestwick and Dean Cross is 134° in one direction and 314° in the opposite direction; the difference between the two is, of course, 180°. For airband listeners, it is often useful to use this information to pinpoint a particular flight. A message that *'We have just passed Dean Cross heading 314'* can only mean that the aircraft is on Amber One heading for Prestwick.

It will be seen that certain airways do not appear on both high altitude and low altitude charts. In some cases only the high altitude airway exists, therefore aircraft below the airway are not under mandatory control of an air traffic control centre.

Explanation of the main airways abbreviations shown on radio navigation charts. Details vary slightly according to the publisher.

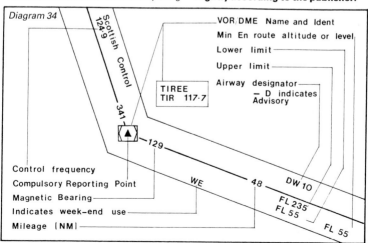

Diagram 34

The distance between VOR beacons is shown alongside the airway in nautical miles. Also shown is the VHF radio frequency for the particular airway, although this cannot be taken as meaning that it will be the only frequency used. Often other alternative frequencies are in operation, and from time to time particular frequencies are changed.

The boundaries between control areas are shown with the information relating to the adjoining areas printed alongside the boundary.

En-route charts produced by Aerad, Jeppesen and the Royal Air Force all show this basic information, but in slightly different versions.

Airways are commonly known by a colour system, Amber, Blue, Green, Red or White, followed by a particular number. The only exception at the time of writing is 'UL1' (Upper Lima One) between Lyneham and Cork, which is a 'link' route used solely by eastbound transatlantic flights between 7pm and 7am. More link routes can be found in other parts of Europe.

Airways are 10-mile wide sections of airspace coming within the jurisdiction of an air traffic controller. Airways join beacons or reporting points in straight lines.

High level airways are prefixed 'U' for Upper — eg 'Upper Green One'. A number of airways running alongside each other may be designated as North, South, East or West. For example, Upper Amber 25 has Upper Amber 25 East on its eastern side. Upper Red One North, Upper Red One South and Upper Red One run roughly alongside each other.

Note that the centre lines of high level and low level airways do not always coincide.

Although aircraft flying above flight level 245 are under positive control, the airspace is not actually controlled airspace but a Special Rules Area.

Diagram 35

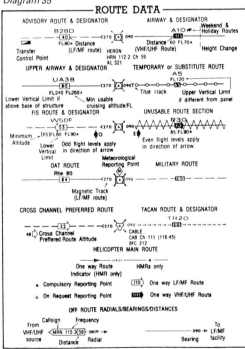

Left and right:
Part of the chart legend produced by the Royal Air Force.

Diagram 36

AERODROMES

◎ ● Military   ◇ ◇ Civil   ◈ ◈ Joint   (H) Helicopter   ◇ Seadrome

Aerodromes shown in grey:- Runway Lengths < 7000ft High Altitude Charts
Lengths < 5000ft Low & High Charts

NAVIGATION AIDS

TACAN	VORTAC	VOR/TACAN	VOR	VOR/DME	DME

✕	⊣⊢	⊙	∘
Consol/NDB/Lctr	BROADCAST STATION	FAN MARKER	LORAN TRANSMITTER EUREKA

Low power MF Beacon shown on grey:- High Altitude Charts < 100nm/100w
Low/High Altitude Charts < 50nm/50w
Those associated with oil & gas installations are by arrangement and shown in magenta.
The following suffixes are shown after frequencies:
A1 to indicate emission of NDB is A1A or A1A/NON. B VOR carries Voice Broadcast.
T Terminal VOR (low power). BT Terminal VOR with Voice Broadcast.

BOUNDARIES

Area of Limited Aeronautical Information	For full information see 'Inset' of area
FIR	UIR	FIR/UIR
SUB-FIR	ASRgn	FWA
TCA/MTCA/TIA	TCA Sector	TCAs Adjoining
SRA	ADA	Corridors
HPZ	SRZ	BUFFER ZONE
UTA/CTA Sector	MCTA/CTA/UTA/OCA	MCTZ/CTZ/TIZ/MATZ/ATZ
Radar Service Area (Mandatory)	Radar Service Area (Advisory)	Radar Sector
ADIZ		International

• • • • • • • • ACC Radio frequency boundary
• • • • • • • ACC/TCA Radio frequency sector
• • • • • ACC/TCA Radio frequency sub-sector

• • • • • • • • FIC Radio frequency boundary
• • • • • • • FIC Radio frequency sector
• • • • • FIC Radio frequency sub-sector

Whilst this chapter attempts to explain the variety of charts and other types of information available, there is, of course, no substitute for the real thing. Anyone with an interest in air traffic control, or aviation generally, should try and obtain at least some of the more popular publications — you won't be disappointed! In any case, because of the size of this book, it would not be possible to show clearly the many airways and navigation beacons of UK airspace and readers are advised to purchase their own copies of radio navigation charts.

6 Arrivals and Departures

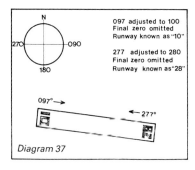

Diagram 37

The complexity of airport operations is directly related to the type and volume of traffic handled and although in all cases the basic procedures remain the same, a small provincial airfield dealing only with light aircraft would not be expected to possess the sophisticated aids and facilities of a large scale operation such as Heathrow or Gatwick. Similarly, the number of personnel necessary to provide effective control also increases in proportion to the number of 'movements'. A 'movement' is the method of measuring the volume of traffic at an airport, each landing and take-off counting as a movement.

Above:
Method of describing runways. Heathrow has six runways — 28 left, 28 right, 10 left, 10 right, 05 and 23.

Runways

The runways at an airport are designated according to their compass bearings rounded off to the nearest 10°, with the final zero omitted. For example, a runway which faces almost due west (say 266°) would be rounded off to 270° and described as 'Runway 27'. The same runway, used in the opposite direction, will be facing due east and will differ by 180°, that is 090°. It will then be described as 'Runway 09'. Where two parallel runways are available, as at Heathrow, they are known as 'left' and 'right' respectively, as shown in diagram 37. Occasionally, knowledge of individual runways is helpful to airband listeners, especially where only the aircraft radio transmissions can be heard, since one of the clues to the destination may be the 'runway in use' quoted by the ground controller. Hearing the words 'Willow one Bravo arrival for two six' identified the destination as Gatwick, because Gatwick's runways are designated 26 and 08.

Below:
Diagram of the popular expressions heard in connection with airfield circuits. A final approach of more than 4 miles is described as a Long Final.

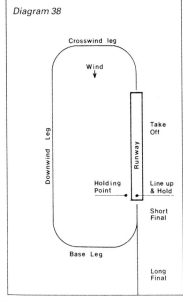

Diagram 38

Categories 1, 2 and 3

Airports provided with an Instrument Landing System (ILS) conform with one of three categories enabling suitably equipped aircraft to land in varying degrees of poor visibility.

The four runways at Heathrow are 'Cat 3' enabling blind landings for suitably equipped aircraft. British Airways are able to claim high reliability for their Shuttle services because all aircraft are Cat 3.

Airfields

A number of terms can be heard in transmissions concerning manoeuvres near airfields, particularly small airfields where the traffic consists mainly of light aircraft. These terms are best explained by means of an illustration. (See diagram 38.) A 'left-hand' circuit is shown, where all turns are to the left; a 'right-hand' pattern would be one where turns are to the right.

Automatic Terminal Information Service (ATIS)

At small airfields information about weather conditions is transmitted directly by the control personnel, but at larger airports such details are often provided by prerecorded tapes broadcast on a continuous basis. At Heathrow, for example, there are separate transmissions for Arrivals and Departures. The Arrival information is identified by letter, changing at regular intervals, and aircraft are requested to indicate the identification letter to Heathrow approach on first radio contact.

A transcript of a typical Heathrow broadcast is as follows:

'This is Heathrow Arrival information Sierra. One four four five weather, one zero five degrees zero nine knots. Cavok. Temperature plus nine, dew point plus four. The QNH one zero two five millibars. Landing runway one zero left. Continuous descent approach is in progress. Report aircraft type and information Sierra received on first contact with Heathrow Approach.'

(NB The expression 'Cavok' is explained in Chapter 9.)

When aircraft contact Heathrow approach the transmission will include the aircraft type and the identification of the Arrival information. For example:

'Heathrow Approach Speedbird six two five, seven three seven with Sierra, eight zero, eight to run to Ockham.'

The flight is BA625, aircraft type Boeing 737, Information Sierra, flight level 80, 8 miles before Ockham reporting point.

A similar broadcast, on a different frequency, can be heard at Heathrow for departures.

'This is Heathrow Departure information Romeo one four one five hours weather. One one five degrees magnetic at one one knots. Temperature plus zero nine dew point zero four. QNH one zero two five millibars. Departure runway one zero right.'

SID's and STAR's

Routes to and from airports are arranged to ensure maximum safety and economy; ATC clearances for departures and arrivals usually relate either to SID's (Standard Instrument Departures) or STAR's (Standard Arrivals). Charts for individual airports provide details of such routes. The transcript of the Wardair flight 411 given later in this chapter includes reference to the standard Manchester departure Dean Cross 60, and this is illustrated and described in diagram 40. Similar charts cover arrivals and departures for other airports

Holding

During busy periods, arriving aircraft may be required to delay their approach because of weather or traffic congestion, and this is known as 'holding'. Various holding patterns are available near main airports, and aircraft fly a racetrack pattern until an approach is possible, or alternatively a decision to divert is made. Standard holding patterns may themselves become congested and in such cases aircraft may be required to hold by flying between navigation beacons, as for example between Lands End and Ibsley in southern England. Holding patterns are sometimes referred to as 'stacks' because aircraft are stacked one above the other with 1,000ft separation. As the lowest flight is cleared to leave the hold, other flights descend in 1,000ft steps. Flights which are required to hold will be requested (for example) to 'Enter the hold at Lambourne'. Full details of holding patterns are given on arrival charts for individual airfields.

Departures

Before departure, passenger or freight carrying aircraft are required to file a flight plan detailing various aspects of the proposed flight. The ATC clearance will be passed to the pilot, when ready, shortly before permission to start the engines and 'push back' is given. The clearance will be sent by land line to the departure airport from the centre at either West Drayton or Prestwick, as appropriate.

Diagram 39
DAVENTRY SIDs
LONDON/ Heathrow

GENERAL INFORMATION
1 SIDs reflect Noise Preferential Routeings.
2 Initial climb straight ahead to 580' QNH (500' QFE).
3 Cross Noise Monitoring Points not below 1080' QNH (1000' QFE) thereafter maintain minimum climb gradient of 4% to 4000' to comply with Noise Abatement requirements.

Gnd speed	kt	75	100	150	200	250	300
4%(244'per nm)	ft/min	305	407	610	813	1017	1220

4 Callsign for RTF frequency use when instructed after take-off 'London Control'.
5 En Route cruising level will be issued after take-off by 'London Control'.
6 Max IAS 250kts below FL100 unless otherwise authorised.

TRANSITION ALT
6000'

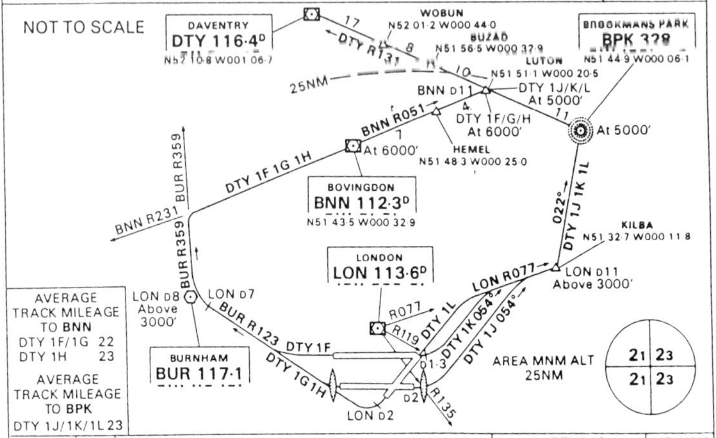

NOT TO SCALE

DAVENTRY
DTY 116·4^D
N52 10·8 W001 06·7

WOBUN
N52 01·2 W000 44·0

BUZAD
N51 56·5 W000 32·9

BROOKMANS PARK
BPK 329
N51 44·9 W000 06·1

DTY R131

LUTON
N51 51·1 W000 20·5

25NM

BNN D11
DTY 1J/K/L
At 5000'

BNN R051

DTY 1F/G/H
At 6000'

At 5000'

DTY 1F 1G 1H

At 6000'

HEMEL
N51 48·3 W000 25·0

BNN R231

BUR R359

BUR R359

BOVINGDON
BNN 112·3^D
N51 43·5 W000 32·9

022°

KILBA
N51 32·7 W000 11·8

LONDON
LON 113·6^D

LON R077

LON D11
Above 3000'

AVERAGE TRACK MILEAGE TO BNN
DTY 1F/1G   22
DTY 1H   23

LON D8
Above 3000'

LON D7

BUR R123

DTY 1F

R077

DTY 1L

DTY 1K 054°

DTY 1J 054°

BURNHAM
BUR 117·1

DTY 1F

DTY 1G 1H

R119 DTY 1L

D1·3

R135

AREA MNM ALT
25NM

21	23
21	23

AVERAGE TRACK MILEAGE TO BPK
DTY 1J/1K/1L 23

LON D2

SID	RWY	ROUTEING(including Noise Preferential Routeing)	ALTITUDES	AIRWAY ROUTE
DTY 1F 128·90	28R	Straight ahead to intercept BUR VOR R123. At LON D7 turn right to follow BUR VOR R359 to intercept R231 to BNN VOR, continue on R051 to LUTON intersection (BNN D11) then turn left to intercept DTY VOR R131 to DTY VOR.	Cross **BUR VOR (LON D8)** above 3000' **BNN VOR and LUTON** intersection at 6000'	A2 A1E B3 B4 W22– Northbound
DTY 1G 128·90	28L	At 10R MM turn right to intercept BUR VOR R123. At LON D7 turn right to follow BUR VOR R359 to intercept R231 to BNN VOR, continue on R051 to LUTON intersection (BNN D11) then turn left to intercept DTY VOR R131 to DTY VOR.		
DTY 1H 128·90	23	At LON D2 turn right to intercept BUR VOR R123. At LON D7 turn right to follow BUR VOR R359 to intercept R231 to BNN VOR, continue on R051 to LUTON intersection (BNN D11) then turn left to intercept DTY VOR R131 to DTY VOR.		
DTY 1J 125·80	10R	At 28L MM (LON VOR R135/D2) turn left to track 054 to intercept LON VOR R077 to KILBA intersection (LON D11) turn left onto QDM 022 to BPK NDB then to DTY VOR.	Cross **KILBA** intersection (LON D11) above 3000' **BPK NDB and LUTON** intersection (DTY VOR R131/D35) at 5000'	
DTY 1K 125·80	10L	At LON VOR R119/D1·3 turn left to track 054 to intercept LON VOR R077 to KILBA intersection (LON D11) turn left onto QDM 022 to BPK NDB then to DTY VOR.		
DTY 1L 125·80	05	Straight ahead to intercept LON VOR R077 to KILBA intersection (LON D11) then turn left onto QDM 022 to BPK NDB then to DTY VOR.		

CHANGE NEW CHART

AERO INF DATE 8 May 86

Left:
Standard Instrument Departure routes via Daventry from London Heathrow. *Civil Aviation Authority*

Right:
Standard Instrument Departure Chart for Manchester International Airport. *Aerad*

Diagram 40

MANCHESTER

DEAN CROSS & POLE HILL **SID's**

Trans alt **4000**		

1. Initial climb. After T/O climb ahead to 500ft QFE before commencing any turn.
2. Communications: Change to S.I.D. Freq (126.65) when advised.
3. Speed Control: Max IAS 250 Kts below FL100 unless otherwise authorised.

G2	G2
	FFF

13 MAY 1982

EGCC

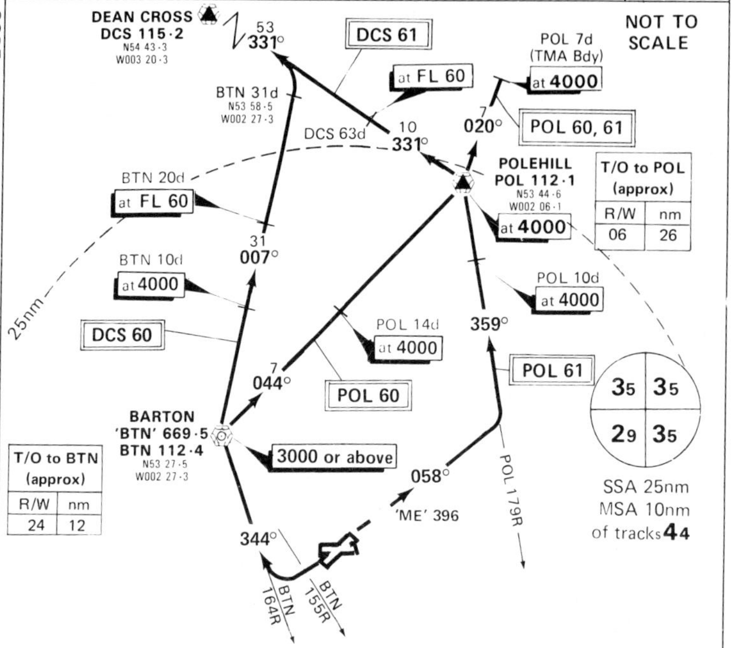

DEAN CROSS DCS 115·2
N54 43·3 W003 20·3

/ 53 331°

DCS 61

at FL 60

POL 7d (TMA Bdy)

at 4000

NOT TO SCALE

BTN 31d N53 58·5 W002 27·3

DCS 63d 10 331°

7 020°

POL 60, 61

BTN 20d POL 20d

at FL 60

POLEHILL POL 112·1
N53 44·6 W002 06·1

at 4000

T/O to POL (approx)	
R/W	nm
06	26

25nm

BTN 10d

at 4000

31 007°

POL 10d

at 4000

DCS 60

POL 14d

at 4000

359°

POL 61

3₅	3₅
2₉	3₅

7 044°

POL 60

BARTON 'BTN' 669·5
BTN 112·4
N53 27·5 W002 27·3

T/O to BTN (approx)	
R/W	nm
24	12

3000 or above

058°

POL 179R

SSA 25nm
MSA 10nm
of tracks **44**

344°

'ME' 396

BTN 164R BTN 155R

SID	R/W	ROUTEING (including Min Noise Routeing)	ALTITUDES
DCS 60	24	At BTN 155R right onto Tr 344M(BTN 164R) to BTN. At BTN right on BTN 007R until at BTN 31d left on Tr 331M(DCS 151R) to DCS	BTN at 3000 or above BTN 007R 10d at 4000 BTN 007R 20d at FL 60
DCS 61	06	Ahead to 'ME' At 'ME' continue on Tr 058M until left onto Tr 359M(POL 179R) to POL. At POL left on POL 331R to DCS.	POL 179R 10d at 4000 POL at 4000 DCS 151R 63d at FL 60.
POL 60	24	At BTN 155R right onto Tr 344M(BTN164R) to BTN. At BTN right on Tr 044M(POL 224R) to POL. At POL left on POL 020R to clear controlled airspace at POL 7d.	BTN at 3000 or above. POL 224R 14d at 4000 POL 020R 7d at 4000.
POL 61	06	Ahead to 'ME'. At 'ME' continue on Tr 058M then left onto Tr 359M(POL 179R) to POL. At POL right on POL 020R to clear controlled airspace at POL 7d.	POL 179R 10d at 4000 POL 020R 7d at 4000

Revision: Facilities

A typical transcript for such a departure from Manchester is given below. Soon after take-off the flight will be handed over to the sector radar controller at the control centre to continue its journey.

AC: *'Manchester Ground, Wardair four one one heavy, gate twenty three, requesting push back clearance and start up.'*

ATC: *'Wardair four one one is cleared to push and start gate twenty three.'*

AC: *'Roger, thank you.'*

AC: *'Wardair four eleven ready to taxi.'*

ATC: *'Four one one holding point two four, your clearance when ready.'*

AC: *'Go ahead, four eleven.'*

ATC: *'Cleared Vancouver Dean Cross six zero departure squawk five five one three, departure frequency one two four decimal two.'*

AC: *'Cleared Vancouver Dean Cross six zero, five five one three, one two four two, thank you.'*

ATC: *'Correct.'*

(Several minutes pass as the aircraft taxies to the runway.)

ATC: *'Wardair four one one continue with the tower one one eight decimal seven goodnight.'*

AC: *'One one eight seven goodnight.'*

(Change of frequency.)

AC: *'Manchester Tower good evening it's Wardair four eleven.'*

ATC: *'Wardair four one one good evening, cleared to the holding point two four.'*

AC: *'Cleared to the holding point two four.'*

ATC: *'Wardair four one one after the landing one eleven line up and wait runway two four.'*

AC: *'Four eleven, after the one eleven line up and wait.'*

ATC: *'Wardair four one one you are cleared take-off runway two four. Surface wind is calm.*

AC: *'Four one one cleared for take-off.'*

(Aircraft takes off.)

ATC: *'Wardair four one one call Manchester one two four decimal two goodnight.'*

AC: *'Roger good day.'*

The departing aircraft continues to climb and will be later transferred to London Control on frequency 131.05. The total time taken for this transcript would be approximately 17 minutes. In practice, messages to several other aircraft would also occur during the same period.

Arrivals

Aircraft arriving at an airport are first transferred to the airport Approach frequency by the ATCC. Airport information may be obtained from recorded messages or directly from the ATC personnel. Aircraft are 'vectored' to a position which places them in line with the landing runway, after which the aircraft will lock on to the ILS radio transmissions. If ILS is not available, a visual approach may be possible, or alternatively a surveillance radar approach will be provided from the control tower.

Flights will have been cleared to a local reporting point, usually an NDB, following which approach control will direct the pilot to a position which will enable an approach to the landing runway. Detailed Arrival information for airports is shown on the appropriate charts, available for every airport.

Heathrow

A flight preparing to depart from London Heathrow will make its first call, requesting start up and route clearance, on frequency 121.7. The pilot will give the call sign, the gate number at which the aircraft is parked, and the code letter of the Automatic Terminal Information Service (ATIS) departure information broadcast which has been received on a separate frequency. This enables the controller to determine the precise weather data to which the pilot is operating and he is then in a position to advise the pilot if the weather information is out of date or if there is likely to be a significant change.

In practice, the use of an airband radio at a busy airport like Heathrow, where there are many radio frequencies in use, can be disappointing if the set does not have crystals to pinpoint each frequency. The 'start up' frequency, on 121.7, is in fact very close to the 'ground' frequency on 121.9 but, more importantly, it is also near the ATIS broadcast on 121.85.

The effect, with a poor quality radio receiver, is that 121.7 and 121.9 may well be swamped by the ATIS transmission. A crystal controlled set can, of course, be tuned in very accurately to the precise frequency and the 'overlapping' effect is thereby eliminated. The controller on 121.7 will give the clearance to start, and the flight plan route for the aircraft, identifying the Standard Instrument Departure (SID) route by its reporting point and signifying letter — for example 'Clacton One Foxtrot' departure. Each SID is shown on the departure charts for the various runways at Heathrow. The controller will also indicate the squawk code for the flight. After the pilot has read back the clearance details, the controller requests a frequency change to 121.9.

The pilot will set the Inertial Navigation System to the appropriate latitude and longitude of the actual stand at which the aircraft is parked and may also check the altimeter by reference to the airfield elevation above mean sea level.

On the Ground Movement frequency of 121.9, traffic (both aircraft and vehicular) on or in the vicinity of the runways is monitored by the controller. The flight, which by now has its engines running, requests clearance to 'push back' and taxi to the departure runway holding point. The controller will issue the clearance, having regard to other aircraft in the area, and the aircraft will taxi out towards the holding point.

On approaching the runway, the Ground Movement Controller will request the pilot to 'monitor' the departure control frequency on 118.5. The aircraft will, in due course, be contacted by the Departure Controller and instructions for the remainder of the taxying and the departure will be given.

Other flights may be required to depart at different points farther down the runway or alternatively some may need the full length of the runway. Eventually, the aircraft will line up on the runway and the take-off clearance will be issued, together with the wind direction and wind speed.

After take-off the departure time is given to the pilot and control is passed to one of the London Terminal Manoeuvring Area Controllers (depending on the route taken) and later to the en-route area control frequency.

Arriving flights are similarly handled by several controllers after handover from LATCC. First contact is on frequency 119.2, with two Approach Controllers working closely together to integrate traffic arriving from the north via Bovingdon and Lambourne, and from Ockham and Biggin to the south. Traffic is arranged into two orderly streams of traffic until the Radar Directors take over. Radio frequency is then changed to 120.4. The aircraft are brought together to form a single stream as they line up with the runway in use, taking into account their relative sizes and speeds. At about six to eight miles from touchdown, the Air Arrivals Controller takes over on 118.7 and gives clearance to land. After landing, responsibility is passed on to the Ground Movement Controller on 121.9.

The following messages illustrate typical activity at London Heathrow during the busy midday period, and covers the transmissions from initial start up of engines through to actual departure. As mentioned earlier the various ATC operations are subdivided among the control staff because of the sheer volume of traffic. The first section is a transcript of frequency 121.7. (In the following section aircraft are indicated as AC, control is indicated as ATC, and road vehicles are indicated as RV.)

(The messages are based on actual transmissions and may not always be in accordance with recognised RT phraseology.)

AC: *Good afternoon Shuttle four Xray start please November forty nine.*

ATC: *Shuttle four Xray, Roger, starts approved clearance is to Belfast, Daventry one Foxtrot squawk five four seven six.*

AC: *Thank you, start approved, Daventry one Foxtrot five four seven six, four Xray.*

ATC: *That's correct one two one nine goodday.*

AC: *Heathrow Swissair eight zero five.*

ATC: *Swissair eight zero five.*

AC: *We have missed our slot, do you have another one about ten minutes later? We can accept all levels up to three seven zero.*

ATC: *Stand by on that eight oh five I'll check for you.*

ATC: *Swissair eight zero five.*

AC: *Go ahead.*

ATC: *Take-off time at four five for you now — time four five.*

AC: *That's fine sir, thank you very much.*

AC: *Ground good afternoon Speedbird*

six three eight is Echo three eight with Whisky for Copenhagen please.

ATC: Speedbird six three eight starts approved Clacton one Foxtrot squawk zero three three seven.

AC: Roger six three eight confirm is cleared to start Clacton one Foxtrot zero three three seven.

ATC: That's correct one two one nine bye.

AC: London good afternoon Lufthansa zero five seven we've got information Whisky and we're at stand Foxtrot two for start.

ATC: Clearance approved zero five seven Dover one Foxtrot for Cologne squawk zero three one three.

AC: Start is approved Cologne Dover one Foxtrot zero three one three on the squawk one two one nine good day.

ATC: Bye now.

AC: Heathrow ground this is Japan Air four two two good afternoon.

ATC: Station calling Heathrow say again call sign.

AC: This is Japan Air four two two, we're starting for Anchorage stand Lima twenty nine Information Xray.

ATC: Japan Air four two two starts approved for Anchorage.

ATC: Japan Air four two two starts approved for Anchorage Daventry one Foxtrot departure squawk five six five zero.

AC: Japan Air four two two, cleared Anchorage Daventry one Foxtrot squawking five six five zero.

ATC: Clearance correct and one two one decimal nine for your pushback goodday.

AC: Japan Air four two two goodday.

AC: Good afternoon Heathrow TWA seven seven one at Lima twenty four with Xray for pushback.

ATC: Transworld seven seven one negative on the pushback — start is approved Daventry one Foxtrot departure Squawk five two four four.

AC: Negative on the pushback — OK to start Daventry one Foxtrot, five two four four.

ATC: Clearance correct and for pushback contact one two one decimal nine goodday.

AC: Goodday.

AC: Heathrow Ground Speedbird two nine seven heavy information Xray Kilo one seven for start up.

ATC: Speedbird two nine seven standby

for start.

AC: Speedbird two nine seven standing by.

ATC: Speedbird two nine seven.

AC: two nine seven go ahead.

ATC: Speedbird two nine seven start up approved Daventry one Foxtrot Squawk five five six six.

AC: Speedbird two nine seven cleared to start Daventry one Foxtrot five five six six.

ATC: Clearance correct, one two one decimal nine.

AC: one two one nine bye.

(Note: In the previous messages the stands or parking bays are identified by letter and number — for example Kilo one seven — and the current Airport Terminal Information Service [ATIS] departure broadcast is referred as Information Whisky, changing to Information Xray during the transcript.)

The radio frequency is now changed to 121.9 to monitor the messages giving the clearances to pushback and to taxi. (Note that arriving aircraft are also on this frequency after actually landing.)

AC: Midland zero five eight taxi.

ATC: Midland zero five eight, on to the outer taxiway for the holding point two eight right.

AC: Standard for two eight right Midland zero five eight.

ATC: Lufthansa zero five seven second right on to the outer taxiway.

AC: Second right onto the outer Lufthansa zero five seven.

ATC: Lufthansa zero five seven monitor one one eight decimal five.

AC: One one eight decimal five, goodbye zero five seven.

AC: Ground good afternoon Finnair eight three three, vacating two three.

ATC: Finnair eight three three good afternoon right turn now for stand Foxtrot two.

AC: Next turn right Fox two, eight three three.

ATC: Midland zero five eight can you accept Block sixteen — it might slightly expedite your departure.

AC: Yes that will be OK Midland zero five eight.

ATC: Roger, hold south of sixteen.

AC: Midland three three six taxi — we can also take sixteen.

ATC: Midland three three six Roger head on the inner taxiway initially — I'd like you to go to the full length — there's a heavy aircraft behind you — won't be able to taxi past.

AC: OK go to the full length three three six.

ATC: Speedbird zero five eight, monitor one one eight decimal five.

AC: One one eight five goodbye.

ATC: Goodbye.

AC: Heathrow ground Speedbird two nine seven heavy Kilo seventeen for pushback please.

ATC: Two nine seven heavy Roger Kilo seventeen pushback approved — face north.

AC: To push, face north Speedbird two nine seven.

ATC: Midland three three six next left on to the outer taxiway — hold behind the company DC nine.

AC: Three three six understood.

AC: Good afternoon ground, six three eight is Echo Thirty eight for push please.

ATC: Speedbird six three eight, Afternoon, pushback approved.

AC: Thank you six three eight.

ATC: Midland three three six Monitor one one eight Decimal five.

AC: One one eight five, Bye.

AC: Heathrow Ground Japan Air four two two requests taxi.

ATC: Japan Air four two two Roger right turn on the inner taxiway holding point two eight right.

AC: Japan Air four two two Roger right turn on the inner, then to the holding point thank you.

RV: Hello ground Lido nine.

ATC: Lido nine pass your message.

RV: Lido nine permission to cross runway two three at block seventy three please.

ATC: Lido nine hold position, call you back.

RV: Lido nine holding position.

AC: Kilo Oscar at runway two three.

ATC: Kilo Oscar hold position, call you back.

AC: Kilo Oscar.

ATC: Kilo Oscar cross runway two three on the northern dual now, report vacated go on to the inner taxiway.

AC: Kilo Oscar.

ATC: Lido nine after the landing one two five cross two three report vacated.

RV: Cross after the landing one two five, Lido nine.

ATC: Varig seven five eight continue to the holding point two eight right.

AC: Roger seven five eight.

AC: Ground good afternoon Golf Tango Sierra Alpha Mike just vacated two three.

ATC: Alpha Mike good afternoon, right turn there onto the inner taxiway stand Delta five six.

AC: Right onto the inner for Delta five six, Alpha Mike.

AC: Kilo Oscar vacating two three.

ATC: Kilo Oscar, Roger.

AC: Ground six three eight, are we cleared to taxi from Echo?

ATC: Six three eight affirmative left onto the inner taxiway for two eight right.

AC: Left on the inner two eight right, six three eight.

ATC: Japan Air four two two, first left on to the outer taxiway.

AC: Japan Air four two two, Roger, left on to the outer.

AC: Ground Speedbird two nine seven, taxi clearance please.

ATC: Speedbird two nine seven Roger, north on the inner taxiway for the holding point two eight right.

AC: North to the holding point two eight right Speedbird two nine seven.

AC: Ground Speedbird six five one clear of two three.

ATC: Speedbird six five one right turn now on to the inner taxiway for Charlie two two check before entering the cul-de-sac.

AC: Right for Charlie twenty two.

ATC: Japan Air four two two continue to the holding point two eight right, monitor one one eight decimal five.

AC: Japan Air four two two Roger.

There is now a change of radio frequency to 118.5MHz, for clearances on the departure runway 28 right.

ATC: Speedbird six zero four, cleared take-off two eight right, two one zero, one five knots.

AC: Roger, we'll be about fifteen seconds.

ATC: Roger, no problem — you are cleared take off two eight right.

ATC: Japan Air four two two hello, after the seven three seven on the runway departs, line up two eight right.

AC: Japan Air, four two two after the seven three seven line up and wait two eight right.

ATC: *Japan Air four two two cleared take off two eight right wind two one zero at two zero knots.*

AC: *Japan Air four two two cleared take off runway two eight right.*

ATC: *Speedbird six zero four airborne at five eight, London one two eight decimal four bye.*

AC: *Two eight four, six Zero four, Cheers.*

ATC: *Japan Air four two two, airborne at zero one, London one two eight decimal nine bye.*

AC: *Japan Air four two two, one two eight decimal nine goodday.*

ATC: *Golf Alpha Victor Mike Yankee, hello, line up block sixteen.*

AC: *Line up block sixteen, Shuttle Mike Yankee.*

AC: *Shuttle Mike Yankee is lining up two eight right.*

ATC: *Mike Yankee.*

ATC: *Golf Alpha Victor Mike Yankee is cleared take-off two eight right the wind is two one zero at fifteen.*

AC: *Cleared take-off Shuttle Mike Yankee.*

ATC: *TWA seven seven one after the British seven five seven departs line up two eight right.*

AC: *After the seven five seven British line up two eight right TWA seven seven one.*

ATC: *Speedbird six two six cleared take-off two eight right two one zero fifteen.*

AC: *Six two six rolling two eight right.*

ATC: *Mike Yankee airborne zero four London one two eight decimal nine bye.*

AC: *One two eight nine goodday Shuttle Mike Yankee.*

ATC: *Speedbird six two six airborne zero five London one three two Zero five bye.*

AC: *One three two Zero five, six two six.*

ATC: *TWA seven seven one cleared take-off two eight right the wind is two two zero at fifteen.*

AC: *TWA seven seven one rolling.*

ATC: *Sabena six Zero six after the TWA departs line up two eight right.*

AC: *After the TWA seven four seven departs line up two eight right Sabena six Zero six.*

ATC: *Speedbird eight five after the Sabena seven three seven departs line up two eight right.*

AC: *Line up two eight right after the Sabena departs Speedbird eight five.*

ATC: *TWA seven seven one airborne at zero six contact London one two eight decimal nine bye bye.*

AC: *One twenty eight nine seven seven one bye.*

After departure, the aircraft will be handed on to the London Air Traffic Control Centre at West Drayton for onward clearance through the London FIR airways system. Note that the words 'take-off' are used exclusively as part of the clearance to actually leave the ground. At all other times the word 'departure' is used.

Arriving flights are monitored on the Distance From Touchdown Indicator (DFTI), a small radar screen, so that aircraft arrive in a safe and orderly stream. Pilots call 'established' when the aircraft is locked on to the Instrument Landing System, and also when the aircraft passes over the 'outer marker', approximately four miles from touchdown, and the middle marker, approximately one mile from touchdown.

The ILS consists of two radio transmissions, the 'localizer' which indicates the centre line of the runway, and the 'glide path', a horizontal beam angled upwards at 3° to provide the correct angle of approach. Instrument Landing Systems (ILS) have been in use for around 40 years, and they tend to be expensive to instal and can be affected by reflections. The aircraft position can only be indicated after it is 'locked on' to the transmissions. A new type of landing aid, the Microwave Landing System (MLS), will gradually replace ILS after 1995.

MLS has three components — the elevation transmitter, the azimuth broadcast and Distance Measuring Equipment. A signal is transmitted which sweeps from left to right in a fan shape, with the runway in the centre. A particular time interval between the signals indicates the centreline of the runway. Shorter intervals mean that the aircraft is too far left, and longer intervals indicate too far right.

The elevation is measured in the same way, except that the beam signal sweeps in a vertical plane.

The advantage of MLS is that aircraft are able to determine their position at any point on either side of the centreline by reference to the DME whereas ILS uses marker beacons on the extended runway centre-line. MLS can also accommodate 200 channels (compared to 40 with ILS) because it uses higher frequencies.

Once on the ground, control passes to

the Ground Movement Controller. If weather conditions are poor, a special radar showing the runways and the aircraft, known as the Aerodrome Surface Movement Indicator (ASMI) is used to direct aircraft to individual stands.

Surveillance Radar Approach

Airfields not equipped with ILS provide a Surveillance Radar Approach which in effect means that aircraft are 'talked down' by local controllers. Flights are vectored to a position in line with the landing runway, and are then given a radar surveillance service to ensure an accurate approach. A typical transcript of such an approach is given below (in this particular example for Bristol a few years ago).

Note that in this example the pressure setting is based on a QNH of 992, thus the vertical distance above mean sea level is quoted as 'altitude'. As Bristol is 600ft amsl, all levels are height above threshold, plus 600ft. If a QFE pressure setting was being used, the term 'height' would be used, and all vertical distances would be 600ft less than those given. (Chapter 4 explains the terms QNH and QFE.)

ATC: *'Aviaco one one nine zero is approaching five miles from touchdown. Begin descent to maintain a three degree glide path. Your heading of two five five is good. How do you read me?'*

AC: *'Two five five the heading. Reading you five.'*

ATC: *'Do not reply to further instructions. Confirmed cleared to land. two five five the heading. Range is four and a half miles, your altitude should be two zero zero feet on a QNH of nine nine two. Closing nicely from right to left. two five five your heading. Wind check one nine zero, three two knots. Range four miles your altitude should be one eight five zero feet. two five five good heading. . . Range three and a half miles your altitude should be one seven zero zero feet on a QNH of nine nine two. . . two five five. . . Coming on to track nicely from the right. Range three miles your altitude should be one five five zero feet. two five five good heading for the moment. . . Turn right five degrees heading two six zero. . . two six zero. . . On track. . . Range two and a half miles your altitude should be one four zero zero feet. Turn right further five degrees heading two six five. . . two six five. . . Wind check one nine zero, two five knots. two six five the heading. Very slightly left, turn right five, heading two seven zero. . . two seven zero. . . Range two miles, your altitude should be one two five zero feet. Left of track but closing. Turn right a further five heading two seven five. . . two seven five. . . Left of track, range one and a half miles. Your altitude should be one one zero zero feet. Left of track but closing. two seven five the heading. Turn left five heading two seven zero. Coming on to track nicely from the left. Range one mile, your altitude should be nine five zero feet. Left a further five heading two six five. On track at three quarters of a mile, wind check one nine zero degrees, three five knots. Cleared to land. On track, heading good. On track at half a mile from touchdown, approach complete, radar out.'*

Above:
A typical view of a control tower VCR (Visual Control Room).
International Aeradio Ltd

Below:
Airport Surface Movement Indicator 18X radar at Gatwick.
Racal Group Services

Above left:
The Racal Avionics ASMI 18X airport surface surveillance system installation at Edinburgh Airport, with inset its high definition scan converted TV display.
Racal Group Services

Above:
The new high power radar at London Heathrow Airport.
Hollandse Signaalapparaten BV

Left:
The supervisor of the visual control room at his desk (left foreground) in the control tower at Heathrow Airport, and the air movement controllers' desks. *CAA*

7 Flying the North Atlantic

A large proportion of the commercial flights which route over Britain are on transatlantic journeys, many from different parts of Europe, and even the Middle East, as well as Britain. The volume of traffic is truly remarkable, although in recent years the fuel crisis and the general fall in demand has resulted in a decrease in the number of flights.

Before 1985, the highest number, in both directions, was recorded in 1978, when 128,000 flights crossed the North Atlantic during the year. This record was exceeded in 1985, with a total volume of 136,500 flights.

Also in 1978, the highest daily traffic volume occurred with more than 300 aircraft flying across the ocean in one direction (westerly) in a single day. Current forecasts predict a dramatic increase in commercial air traffic before the end of the century. The majority of flights for the North Atlantic route through UK airspace, and many can be heard without much difficulty on an airband radio.

Before crossing the Atlantic, however, the pilot must obtain what is known as his 'oceanic clearance', which gives him authority to proceed on a particular route. Oceanic airways differ fundamentally from those across land because they are not fixed in the same way as normal airways.

Routes across the Atlantic, known as 'tracks', are revised twice every 24 hours, once in each direction, and the tracks may vary considerably from day to day. The main consideration for the construction of the daily track system is the weather, with particular attention to the high speed winds known as 'jet streams' which significantly affect the economy of long flights.

Planners on both sides of the Atlantic, at Gander and at Prestwick, Scotland, consult over the daily track construction, with Gander being responsible for the night time tracks, and Prestwick for the day time tracks.

Eastbound tracks are valid between 01.00 and 08.00 GMT, and westbound tracks are valid between 11.30 and 19.00 GMT. (In both cases the times apply at 30° west.)

Details of the daily track system are passed directly to airlines who regularly use the Atlantic and to airports which are situated close to the oceanic boundary. In addition, the track co-ordinates are broadcast on frequency 133.80 in the VHF airband range. If you are in some parts of the United Kingdom it is quite likely that the continuous broadcast will be heard on a normal airband radio, between 09.00 and 19.00 GMT every day, giving details of the westbound tracks.

The boundary between oceanic airspace and the UK and Shannon FIR's is shown on AERAD chart Nat 1/2, which also covers the whole of the North Atlantic. The boundary crosses below southern Ireland, then to the west of Ireland, then to the west of Scotland, and is shown in diagram 41. The actual entry/exit points to the oceanic control area coincide with whole degrees of latitude and longitude, as follows:

49° North 8° West	55° North 10° West
50° North 8° West	56° North 10° West
51° North 8° West	57° North 10° West
51° North 15° West	58° North 10° West
52° North 15° West	59° North 10° West
53° North 15° West	60° North 10° West
54° North 15° West	61° North 10° West

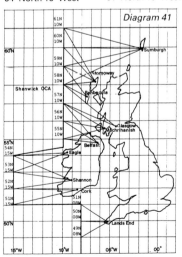

Diagram 41

Chart showing the Entry Points for the Shanwick Oceanic Control Area.
Produced from information supplied by National Air Traffic Services

72

These points can be plotted on a normal world atlas or (even better) on a globe. The advantage of a globe is that it can be used to show direct lines between two points on the earth's surface (known as 'great circle' routes) and it is then easy to appreciate that, for example, a straight line between Paris and Los Angeles takes a flight in a northerly direction over Scotland.

The other difference between 'Oceanic' and 'Domestic' (the term often used to refer to airways control over land) is that the radio frequencies used to obtain oceanic clearances do not have any relation to the different frequencies used when flying on airways. In other words, irrespective of location, an aircraft requesting oceanic clearance will always use one of two frequencies, either 123.95MHz or 127.65MHz. The first is used by aircraft registered west of 30°W, the second by aircraft registered east of 30°W. In practice the effect of this generally means that British and European airlines use 127.65 and American and Canadian airlines use 123.95.

On our side of the Atlantic, the clearances for aircraft to use particular oceanic tracks are obtained from Prestwick airport, the home of the Oceanic Area Control Centre, known as 'Shanwick', a combination of *Shan*non and Prest*wick*. Several tracks are arranged each day, and the westerly group is lettered 'Alpha', 'Bravo', 'Charlie' and so on, with 'Alpha' being the most northerly. A typical North Atlantic organised track system is shown in diagram 42.

The daily decisions regarding track positions depend so much on the prevailing weather conditions that wide variations can be seen throughout the year.

In all cases, the most northerly westbound track is identified as Track Alpha, irrespective of its position. Where Track Alpha commences, for example, at 52° North 15° West, then Track Bravo will commence at 51°N 08°W, Track Charlie at 50°N 08°W, and Track Delta at 49°N 08°W. Thus only four tracks will be available in Shanwick airspace and it follows that most flights will transit the southern half of the London Upper Flight Information Region. In different conditions the most northerly entry point could be 61° North 10° West (for Track Alpha) with Bravo at 60°N 10°W, Charlie at 59°N 10°W and so on. The most southerly entry point may then be at 53°N 15°W for Track Juliett.

However, depending upon the weather system at the time, and particularly the jet stream situation, the track entry points may not be consecutive, with certain intermediate entry points being omitted from the track arrangement. Such an example is as follows: Track Alpha 61°N 10°W; Track Bravo 60°N 10°W; Track Charlie 59°N 10°W; Track Delta 58°N 10°W, Track Echo 57°N 10°W; Track Golf 56°N 10°W, Track Hotel 50°N 08°W, Track Juliett 49°N 08°W. It can be seen that the entry points between 56°N 10°W and 50°N 8°W have not been included in the daily track system.

On rare occasions when French airspace is closed (for example, during industrial action) certain flights which would normally route across northwest France may be permitted to route through the Shanwick OCA en-route for Spanish and Portuguese destinations. This allows the flights to continue their journeys outside the French control area, but aircraft must of course be suitably equipped for oceanic navigation.

It is a good idea to listen to the North Atlantic Westbound Track broadcast on frequency 133.80MHz) every day to get some idea of the weather system. Northerly tracks indicate that the prevailing westerly winds are greatest in the southern approaches, and that most Altantic flights to the USA and Canada will avoid the southern UK. Conversely, of course, it also means that eastbound flights will have chosen southerly tracks so that the southwest of England and South Wales will be busy during the early morning.

When the tracks are predominately organised in the southern part of the UK, indicating that northern weather conditions are less suitable, then most UK and European flights will route across the English Channel and the southern half of the UK and Ireland.

The airspace over most of the North Atlantic between 27,500ft and 40,000ft is known as MNPS airspace (Minimum Navigation Performance Specification airspace) and aircraft are required to satisfy certain criteria concerning navigation capabilities. It is obviously very important that aircraft which are out of radar contact must be able to navigate with a very high degree of reliability — the airspace is extremely congested. Diagram 43 show the traffic on a typical day, by no means the busiest.

After departure, when the aircraft is at a

Diagram 42

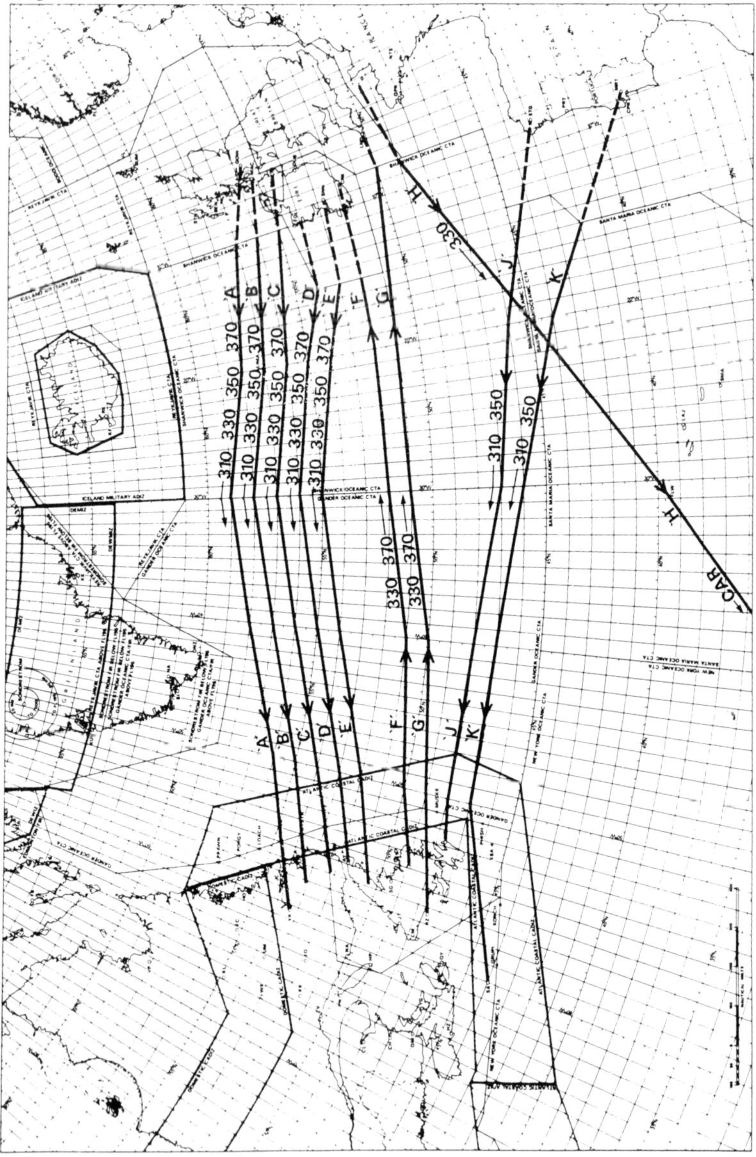

EXAMPLE OF DAY-TIME WESTBOUND ORGANISED TRACK SYSTEM

Typical westbound tracks across the North Atlantic.
Produced from information supplied by National Air Traffic Services

height which will enable radio contact, the aircrew will call 'Shanwick' on one of the two frequencies mentioned earlier. The second radio will be used (often referred to as the 'number two box' both by aircrew and ATC). Naturally Shanwick will have details of the flight and the requested track shown on the flight plan. A typical example of a request for oceanic clearance is given later. Remember that such broadcasts can be heard anywhere in the UK — transatlantic traffic crosses virtually all areas of the country so that radio reception is almost guaranteed. Clearances are transmitted from remote VHF radio stations at Dundonald Hill (Scotland) and at Davidstow Moor in Cornwall. Sometimes aircrew will mention their point of departure in the broadcast, and (more likely) the destination will be quoted. Also, the entry point will be given at the beginning of the message, thus giving the listener a strong lead to the location of the flight. For example, a point of entry of 50° North and 08° West, being west of Lands End, indicates the position of the flight in the south-west of England/English Channel area.

Some of the destination points may not be easily understood, simply because aircrew may refer to airports by their local names. For example, oceanic clearances to 'Kennedy' or to 'Mirabelle' are for New York and Montreal respectively. To fully understand all the various names you will need a suitable reference book on airports or a selection of airline timetables.

The busiest period for hearing oceanic clearances is between 11.00 and 15.00, when many flights will be calling for their track confirmation. It is unlikely that the replies from Shanwick will be received in most parts of the United Kingdom, but as the clearances are invariably read back in full by the aircrew there should be no problem in understanding the details.

After the initial clearance is requested, several minutes will pass before Shanwick recalls the flight. The track co-ordinates will then be passed to the aircraft, and details are read back by the aircrew. Some of the requested tracks, however, may not be available, for a variety of reasons, and alternative flight levels, or even a change of track, may be offered. Occasionally the 'bargaining' may continue for some time before an acceptable route is agreed between the pilot and Shanwick.

Below:

The North Atlantic jet traffic situation at 15.00 hours on 23 July, 1973. Each letter 'A' represents a jet flight.
Produced from information supplied by National Air Traffic Services

Diagram 43

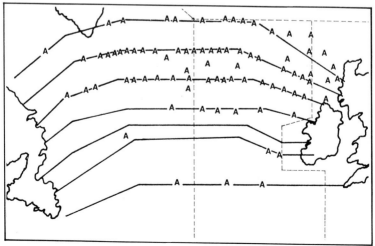

On rare occasions a flight may have to delay its journey by circling in UK airspace, simply because all available tracks are fully committed.

The oceanic clearance will specify the track by its appropriate code letter, the flight level (including any en route changes) the track co-ordinates, and the cleared Mach number. Approximately one flight every hour will be asked to send meteorological reports as it progresses on its journey, referred to as 'SEND MET'.

Before preparing the flight plan, due consideration is given to the various available tracks, and the final choice is that which provides the most suitable route. It follows, therefore, that regular flights may choose several different tracks throughout the year, depending on the suitability of the various available routes. This means that although a particular flight may regularly cross the UK on a particular airway it is inevitable that now and then a different track will be chosen when conditions are suitable. The same applies to inbound flights from the other side of the Atlantic. Don't be surprised, therefore, if a regular flight which always seems to arrive or depart on a particular airway is suddenly absent — it is probably routeing to or from a different oceanic entry point.

For Atlantic crossings, relative speed between aircraft is referred to by Mach numbers, the ratio of the aircraft speed compared to the speed of sound at a particular flight level. (Mach .75 would be three quarters the speed of sound, for example.) Two aircraft, at the same flight level, experiencing the same conditions of wind speed and temperature are more likely to maintain safe separation if they both use the same Mach number. Part of the Shanwick clearance will specify the Mach number to be maintained.

Navigation across the Atlantic is achieved by use of the Inertial Navigation System, of which there are three sets on board. The various co-ordinates of the track are fed into the INS, with the first position being the departure airport. INS is so accurate that each separate parking bay at the airport has its own latitude and longitude, sometimes painted on the bay where it is visible from the cockpit.

Because of the problems of VHF transmissions over long distances, flights over oceanic areas use High Frequency radio (which is not covered in this book).

'Domestic' ATC can be heard to direct aircraft to 'continue with Shanwick on HF' as the flight approaches the oceanic entry point. During the Atlantic crossing, the aircrew may discontinue maintaining a 'listening watch' on the aircraft radio. Instead, the flight may be contacted from the ground radio station by means of a selective calling system, known as 'Selcal'. If the ground station wishes to make contact, a coded radio signal is transmitted to the aircraft. Each flight has its own individual code, and on receipt by the aircraft's decoder a flashing light and/or a chime signal operates on the flight deck, thereby alerting the crew, who will then reply to the ground station using conventional voice transmissions. Selcal removes the necessity for maintaining a continuous listening watch, particularly onerous on lengthy journeys.

To summarise, many interesting transatlantic flights can be heard throughout the UK, by listening-in on either of the oceanic clearance frequencies. Tune in during the busy mid-day period, but have a pencil and paper handy. Write down the co-ordinates of the cleared tracks and plot them on a globe or an atlas. The details are spoken very rapidly, however, and it is quite likely that they will not be easily understood, so a tape recorder will prove invaluable in such instances.

Wherever you happen to be, oceanic clearances can be heard, thus providing a constant source of interest to the enthusiast.

One final point concerns Concorde. Both the French and British SST flights to America have special fixed tracks, detailed in Chapter 8. Both airlines generally use 127.65MHz for confirmation of their oceanic tracks.

The following transcripts are taken from typical broadcasts concerning the North Atlantic track system.

The first is the continuous broadcast heard on 133.8. In this example the most northerly track happens to commence at 52° North and 15° West, therefore the majority of aircraft will route only across the south of England and Wales.

'This is Shanwick. The North Atlantic organised tracks for the twenty seventh of December nineteen eighty three from twelve hundred to nineteen hundred GMT are as follows:

'Track Alpha five two north one five west, five two north two zero west, five two north three zero west, five two north four zero west, five two north five zero west, St Anthony.

'Track Bravo five zero north zero eight west, five one north two zero west, five one north three zero west five one north four zero west five zero north five zero west, Gander.

'Track Charlie four nine north zero eight west, five zero north two zero west, five zero north three zero west, four nine north four zero west, four seven north five zero west, Color.

'Track Delta four eight north zero eight west, four nine north two zero west four nine north three zero west, four eight north four zero west four six north five zero west, Bancs.

'This is Shanwick. Good day.'

The next transcript is for a TWA flight from Heathrow to Chicago, requesting clearance for the oceanic crossing.

AC: 'Shanwick TWA's seven seven one requesting clearance.'

ATC: 'TWA seven seven one go ahead.'

AC: 'TWA seven seven one estimating Belfast one three four three, five six north one zero west one four zero seven, requesting flight level three five zero Mach eight four cruise.'

(The request for TWA 771 indicates an estimate for Belfast VOR at time 13.43, 56°N 10°W at time 14.07. Flight level 35 0 speed Mach 0.84.)

After considering the request, Shanwick calls the aircraft and passes details of the approved clearance. On completion of the transmission, TWA 771 reads back the clearance.

AC: 'TWA seven seven one is cleared to Chicago O'Hare by track Delta, maintain three five zero Mach eight four cruise. Track Delta is five six north, one zero west, five seven north two zero west, five seven north three zero west, five five north four zero west, five three north five zero west, St Anthony. Good day.'

The latitudes and longitudes of the track can be plotted on a globe or atlas. The 'landfall' in this case is St Anthony in Newfoundland. In these two examples, compare the difference between the Track Delta co-ordinates. They illustrate the large variations in North Atlantic tracks for different days.

Boeing 747-136 G-AWNO of British Airways. *BA*

8 Concorde – special arrangements

Few people, even if they are only remotely interested in aviation, can fail to be excited by their first sight of Concorde. The western world's first supersonic transport plane has caught the imagination of the ordinary public like no other, yet its commercial operation has become routine in the space of a few years. At the time of writing, 34 British Airways Scheduled passenger flights cross the Atlantic every week, 28 of them to and from New York, the remainder to and from Washington. In addition, 'pleasure' flights on Concorde are being arranged more and more frequently, perhaps to European or Middle East destinations, or to the Bay of Biscay for a short supersonic trip before returning to London. Air France scheduled Concorde Services to the United States also operate daily, routeing through UK airspace under the control of the London ATCC.

Although Concorde is designed for supersonic flight, it is restricted to normal subsonic speeds and flight levels while over land, to avoid possible disturbance to persons and property on the ground. However, the essential advantage Concorde has over conventional aircraft is the reduction, by roughly fifty per cent, in travelling time between international airports. To ensure that terminal to terminal times are kept to a minimum, Concorde is often given some degree of priority by airport controllers. It is common practice for British Airways Concordes to be

Diagram 44

allowed to 'jump the queue' of departing aircraft, lined up on the taxiways waiting to take off, thus saving several valuable minutes in travelling time. Also, Concorde flights to the United States invariably use runways 28R or 28L (ie the runways which face west) so that their flight is not unnecessarily delayed by the need to turn the aircraft on to the correct heading.

After departure, Concorde flights from Heathrow to the USA follow the Standard Brecon departure route as far as Lyneham in Wiltshire, after which the route is to the Acceleration point, just south of Swansea in the Bristol Channel. The route takes Concorde from Heathrow, over Reading, Lyneham, Bristol (to the north), Newport (in South Wales), Cardiff and then down the Bristol Channel at 28,000ft. South of Swansea the speed is increased and the aircraft climbs to its cruising level of between 55,000ft and 60,000ft.

Immediately after departure from Heathrow, control is passed from Heathrow to the London ATCC at West Drayton, usually on frequency 132.80 or 133.60 (although occasionally 132.60 is used). Shortly after passing Lyneham, and when flight level 280 is reached, control is transferred to London on 132.60.

Right:
Part of the airways chart for SST routes on the North Atlantic produced by Jeppesen for British Airways. *Jeppesen*

Below:
Legend for the SST chart by Jeppesen.

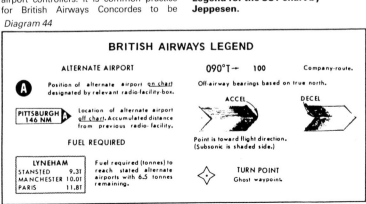

BRITISH AIRWAYS LEGEND

ALTERNATE AIRPORT

A Position of alternate airport <u>on chart</u> designated by relevant radio-facility-box.

PITTSBURGH A
146 NM Location of alternate airport <u>off chart</u>. Accumulated distance from previous radio-facility.

FUEL REQUIRED

LYNEHAM	
STANSTED	9.3T
MANCHESTER	10.0T
PARIS	11.8T

Fuel required (tonnes) to reach stated alternate airports with 6.5 tonnes remaining.

090°T → 100   Company-route.

Off-airway bearings based on true north.

ACCEL   DECEL

Point is toward flight direction. (Subsonic is shaded side.)

TURN POINT
Ghost waypoint.

78

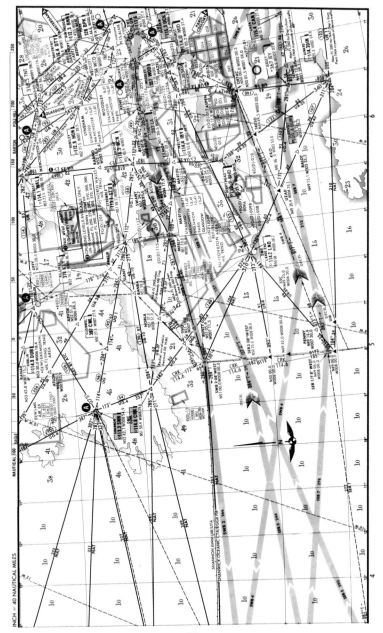

After passing 8° West, the oceanic entry point, control is passed to Shanwick, on High Frequency radio.

During the first part of the flight, before the acceleration point, Shanwick Oceanic Control Centre at Prestwick will be contacted on the aircraft second radio on frequency 127.65 for oceanic clearance, in common with all other transatlantic flights. However, the allocated track will not be one of the usual NAT routes described in Chapter 7. Concorde has special tracks, known as 'Sierra Mike' westbound and 'Sierra November' eastbound. The tracks are shown on diagram 45.

On the return journey, London ATCC will first be contacted on 132.60 when the flight approaches 50°N 8°W, at which time it will be given details of its clearance to Heathrow. Clearance for descent is usually given from its cruising level to 37,000ft and after passing over South Wales, a frequency change is made to either 132.80 or 133.60.

If traffic arrangements are suitable, and ATC authority is given, it may be possible to give the flight permission for a 'straight-in' arrival, which means that the aircraft is able to simply descend, more or less in a straight line, until it approaches the runway at Heathrow, and lands without the usual requirement to follow the normal arrival procedure of routeing via one of the four reporting points for flights to Heathrow. A 'straight-in' will, of course, save several minutes in total travel time and for Concorde is particularly important.

Air France Concorde flights to the United States depart from Charles de Gaulle airport in Paris, and enter UK airspace at the FIR boundary in the English Channel, usually on frequency 134.45 (or alternatively on 127.70). As the flight routes westwards down the English Channel, control is transferred to London on 132.60, and later to the Shanwick Oceanic Control Centre when the flight reaches the oceanic boundary.

Details of times and flight numbers (call-signs) can be found in British Airways and Air France international timetables.

British Airways flights have the special call-sign 'Speedbird Concorde' followed by the flight number. Details can be found in current BA timetables.

The oceanic tracks used by Concorde do not vary as they do for conventional subsonic flights. It is, therefore, not necessary for Concorde to request detailed clearances before entering Oceanic airspace. The transmission to Shanwick is confined to confirming the entry point, with track details in an abbreviated form.

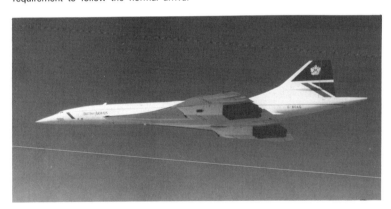

BAe Concorde G-BOAG of British Airways. *BA*

9 London Volmet Service

It is essential for pilots of aircraft to be provided with accurate and up-to-date information on the weather at their destination airfield. In addition, knowledge of conditions at other airfields is required whenever there is a possibility of a diversion from the original destination.

In the majority of cases, including many provincial airports, details of conditions are, on request, passed directly to aircraft by ATC personnel. Information is also available through the FIS (Flight Information Service) for any airfield, the usual method used by aircraft out of radio range from the airfield in question. However, the volume of traffic using the main UK and European airports makes it impractical to pass directly to every flight the weather information currently in force. Instead a pre-recorded message providing such details in a standardised form is broadcast for the main UK and some European airports from Heathrow airport in London. The service is known as 'Volmet', derived from the French word 'Vol', meaning weather.

There are three separate broadcasts, on different VHF radio frequencies:

London Volmet North — 126.600MHz
London Volmet South — 128.600MHz
London Volmet Main — 135.375MHz

Depending on where you live you may be able to hear one or two of these continuous transmissions.

Volmet 'North' is transmitted from Great Dunn Fell. 'South' and 'Main' are both transmitted simultaneously from Davidstow Moor, Ventnor (Isle of Wight), and Warlingham.

Before 1981, weather broadcasts from major world airports were read over the air by local persons. Because of local accents there were sometimes difficulties in clearly understanding the transmissions.

Marconi Space and Defence Systems developed Automatic Volmet to overcome this problem, and since May, 1981 it has been operational from Heathrow. The Marketing Manager of Marconi, Mr John West, has recorded all the standard weather report phrases, words and figures which are digitized and stored in a computer memory.

If you are able to listen in to Volmet, it will not be apparent that the voice is in fact a composite selection of recordings specially prepared for every possible situation. The transmission is almost identical to a normal spoken broadcast, with each word having been recorded in a typical sentence and then fitted to every other word that it could be used with. For example, the same words spoken during a sentence and at the end of a sentence will sound different, with stress being applied to a greater or lesser degree. Periods of silence between words and sentences are also provided for.

The weather reports received at Heathrow are automatically processed and converted into a code which then selects the appropriate phrases from the memory ready for transmission. Although it is a human voice which is heard, the whole process is fully automatic and operates on a continuous basis. The RAF also use this system. Volmet meteorological messages are known as METAR — routine met aerodrome reports. Other types of messages are used for different purposes.

Volmet Main and Volmet South provide information for major airports in the south of England, and also include Pairs (Charles de Gaulle), Paris (Orly), Amsterdam and Brussels.

Volmet North covers airports in the Midlands, the north of England and Scotland, and also includes Heathrow.

Each broadcast consists of the following details in respect of each airport:

a) Station name;
b) Time of observation;
c) Surface wind details;
d) Horizontal visibility;
e) Runway visual range;
f) Weather details;
g) Cloud details;
h) Temperature;
i) Dew point;
j) QNH;
k) Trend

a) The name by which the airport is commonly known;
b) The time of the observation in GMT;
c) The direction of the surface wind and the speed, eg 'Zero seven zero degrees one five knots';

d) Below 5,000 metres the visibility is expressed in metres (eg 'Four zero zero metres'). Above 5,000 metres it is given in kilometres;

e) Runway visual range is given in metres (eg 'five zero zero metres'). Where more than one runway is in use, separate RVR readings may be quoted;

f) Where appropriate, a description of certain weather conditions is given in plain language, eg rain showers, freezing rain, etc;

g) Where applicable, the extent to which the sky is obscured by cloud is given, estimated in eighths of sky covered, known as 'OKTAS', eg 'six Okta one five zero zero feet';

h) Temperature is given in degrees celsius;

i) Dew point is given in degrees celsius;

j) QNH is given in millibars. (For details on QNH refer to Chapter 4);

k) The trend of the weather conditions may be added if a change is expected soon. If no change is expected, an abbreviation of the words 'no significant change' is given, pronounced 'no-sig'.

Where significant changes are expected, one of the following will be heard:

'Gradu' — the change is expected at a constant rate;

'Rapid' — the change is expected in a short period of less than thirty minutes;

'Tempo' — the change is expected to last for less than one hour;

'Inter' — frequent changes are expected, fluctuating almost constantly;

'Tend' — a change is anticipated but it is expected to occur slowly throughout the period.

In conditions where visibility is more than 10 kilometres, the lowest cloud is at a minimum of 5,000ft, there is no cumulonimbus cloud, and there is no precipitation, thunderstorm, shallow fog or low drifting snow, then the relevant parts of the Volmet transmission will be replaced by the expression 'Cavok' derived from 'Cloud And Visibility OK' and pronounced 'KAV-O-KAY'.

A typical broadcast, when conditions are good, is as follows:

'This is London Volmet South, this is London Volmet South. London Heathrow at one four five zero. One zero zero degrees nine knots. Cavok. Temperature nine dewpoint four. QNH one zero two five. Nosig.'

A more complicated transmission, in less favourable conditions, might be:

'Paris Charles de Gaulle at zero seven three zero. Zero eight zero, zero one knots, zero zero five zero metres. Runway visual range zero seven five metres. Fog. Sky obscured. Temperature three, dew point three. QNH one zero two three. Fog dispersal operations are in progress. Gradu. Zero four zero zero metres. Fog. Eight Octa below one zero zero feet.

10 Eurocontrol

The United Kingdom is one of the original states which participated in the formation of Eurocontrol, the European Organisation for the Safety of Air Navigation, which has its headquarters in Brussels.

When Eurocontrol was set up in 1960 five other states were also signatories to the convention, namely Belgium, Germany, France, Luxembourg and the Netherlands. Later, in 1965, Ireland also became a member state. On 1 January, 1986, Portugal became the eighth Member State of Eurocontrol. The basic aims of the organisation are to ensure the safety of air navigation and to secure an orderly and rapid flow of air traffic in the Eurocontrol area.

In addition to the headquarters in Brussels, Eurocontrol also has several centres in other European countries.

Eurocontrol's functions include investigation and determination of common methods of operation and procedures applied by member states, rationalisation of control systems, air traffic services and evaluation of future ATC radars, navigation systems and computers. Other responsibilities include the forward planning for future ATC needs, research and trials, standardisation of facilities, statistics and the training of ATC personnel.

Route charges for ATC services are levied and collected from carriers using Eurocontrol upper airspace, and because this is likely to be of particular interest to enthusiasts, further details are given later in this chapter.

Control Centres

The first international Upper Area Control Centre was established at Maastricht, in Netherlands, by Eurocontrol in 1972. The centre is highly sophisticated with modern systems capable of handling 250 aircraft from more than 30 operating positions. The centre covers upper airspace in Germany, Netherlands, Belgium and Luxembourg.

In 1975 a further centre, designed and supervised by Eurocontrol, was built at Shannon, and in 1977 a third ATC centre, at Karlsruhe, in Germany, was commissioned.

Collection of Route Charges

In 1971 arrangements were introduced for the payment of route charges for flights in the Eurocontrol area. Before this date the responsibility for the payment of costs relating to the provision of air traffic services remained with the governments of individual states, mainly because such facilities were deemed to be a national responsibility, and in addition the services were used by military traffic. However, it was accepted that with the increase in civil aviation traffic after the war the responsibility for funding the entire cost could no longer be borne by national exchequers. The view was also taken that individual carriers should in any case bear some of the costs of providing such facilities.

In addition to the original seven states, agreement was reached with Austria, Portugal, Switzerland and Spain for Eurocontrol to collect route charges on their behalf.

The route charges system provides for a single charge to be made in respect of each flight made within the airspace of any of the participating states, even though the flight may have been made over more than one country. In other words, separate states overflown do not result in separate charges. The information to enable the charges to be calculated is derived from details supplied to Eurocontrol in Brussels by the airlines. Details of flights are obtained from flight plans or flight progress strips, and include dates and times of flights, points of departure and destination (or points of entry into and exit from relevant airspace) aircraft types and the operators' identities. Information concerning scheduled flights is also provided by Eurocontrol to avoid the task of dealing with every flight separately. The data supplied by operators is revised every year. As an indication of the complexity of the system, 44,000 aerodrome 'pairs' were contained on file in 1978, providing information on routes and distances concerning the states involved.

Day-by-day returns are produced listing the various flights for each operator. These are totalled on a monthly basis, and distributed to the airlines.

In 1980, the Central Route Charges Office issued charges amounting to $550,000,000. 85% of charges are paid within four months of the date of issue, with a total recovery of 99%.

Certain flights are not liable for Eurocontrol charges, and these mainly consist of the following:

All VFR flights, military traffic, search and rescue flights and flights concerning the testing and checking of aircraft or air traffic facilities.

Briefly, the method of arriving at the charge to be levied in respect of each flight is as follows:

1 The shortest ('great circle') distance, in kilometres, is obtained between the point of entry into Eurocontrol airspace and the point of exit. In practice the most frequently used route is taken. Where the departure point or the destination is within the Eurocontrol area, then the distance is taken from or to that point, but for each take-off or landing 20 kilometres are deducted to allow for facilities provided by the particular airport authorities. The distance thus obtained is divided by 100, to give the 'distance factor'.

2 The official MATO (maximum take off weight) in metric tons is divided by 50, and the square root of the result is calculated to obtain the 'weight factor'.

3 Multiply item 1 by item 2. This gives the number of 'service units'.

4 The number of 'service units', multiplied by the service unit rate, produces the charge made to the operator. The service unit rate is established annually by the Central Route Charges Office.

Two examples of actual charges which would be levied are set out below, costed on charges which became effective on 1 January, 1986.

The first is for a British Airways BAC 1-11 from Glasgow to Paris Charles de Gaulle.

Service Unit for UK airspace: $54.31
Distance Factor: 6.80
Weight Factor: 0.91
Charge for UK airspace:
 $54.31×6.80×.91=$336.07
Service Unit rate for French airspace:
 $40.16
Distance Factor: 1.81
Weight Factor: 0.91
Charge for French airspace:
 $40.16×1.81×.91=$66.15
Total charge is $336.07+$66.15=$402.22

The second example is for a KLM B747 from New York to Amsterdam, entering UK airspace at 50° North and 8° West.

Service Unit rate for UK airspace $54.31
Distance Factor: 8.00
Weight Factor: 2.69
Charge for UK airspace:
 $54.31×8.00×2.69=$1168.75
Service Unit rate for Netherlands airspace:
 $22.31
Distance Factor: 1.22
Weight Factor: 2.69
Charge for Netherlands airspace:
 $22.31×1.22×2.69=$73.22
Total charge is $1,168.75+
 $73.22=$1,241.97

(It can be seen that there is a considerable difference in the total charges, compared with the same examples quoted in the first edition of this book, especially when the effects of inflation are taken into account.)

In due course each airline will receive an account for these flights and all other flights in airspace in the Eurocontrol area. In addition, of course, are airport charges which are payable to the airport authority.

(A leaflet explaining the fees for airports controlled by the British Airports Authority is available from BAA Head Office at Gatwick Airport.)

11 'Company' Transmissions

Many of the transmissions which can be heard on an airband radio concern messages between aircrew and their handling agencies on the ground. These are known as 'company' messages and in almost every case the frequencies used will be between 129.00MHz and 132.00MHz.

Most major airlines have a base at international airports, each with a specific radio frequency, and pilots are able to speak to their company personnel about their flight.

Although the frequencies are within the VHF airband range, company transmissions are unrelated to Air Traffic Control broadcasts and pilots usually speak to their ground base on the aircraft's second radio.

Also, because they are not connected with ATC or the airways system, company transmissions can be heard in most parts of the UK, although the replies from the ground can only be received if the radio is within range of the base, which will invariably be situated at an airport.

As mentioned earlier, most of the large carriers have company offices at major airports, but some airlines, who perhaps do not operate the volume of traffic to justify a local office, use the facilities of other airlines on an agency basis. Air New

Zealand and South African Airways, for example, use British Airways as their handling agent at Heathrow.

It is often necessary for pilots to be in contact with both their own organisation at their base airport, and with the handling company at the destination airport.

Most Britannia flights, for example, will be in touch with 'Britannia Operations' at Luton, British Midland with BDOps at Castle Donington and so on.

Larger companies may have their operations sub-divided for different purposes; British Airways at Heathrow has separate sections in respect of Operations ('Speedbird Control'), Technical matters ('Speedbird Tech') and Documentation, maps, etc. ('Speedbird Library'). Shuttle flights also use a separate company frequency.

British Airways, for example, uses 131.9MHz, Shuttle flights use 131.8, Pan American uses 131.4, TWA uses 131.6, Dan Air is on 130.65, Aer Lingus is 131.75 and so on.

Many airlines, including some of the large ones, find it uneconomical to maintain a local office at individual airports, but prefer to employ the facilities of a handling company.

One of the largest in the United Kingdom is Servisair, with offices at most airports, and its Head Office at Stockport. Servisair was established more than 30 years ago, and now handles 7½ million passengers a year from 150 airlines. Such companies provide a complete service to the airlines and their passengers, and Servisair in particular can be heard regularly on company frequencies.

Servisair company transmissions are all on the same frequency (130.6MHz) for the following airports: Aberdeen, Belfast, Blackpool, Bristol, Cardiff-Wales, East Midlands, Edinburgh, Exeter, Glasgow, Guernsey, Humberside, Jersey, Leeds/Bradford, Liverpool, Manchester, Newcastle, Stansted, Tees-side. The call sign will include the name of the location — for example, 'Servisair Jersey'.

There are no special procedures for company messages, as there is for ATC but nevertheless a number of expressions and abbreviations have developed and later in the chapter some of the more popular ones are explained. Most transmissions concern the organisational details for the aircraft, its crew, passengers and other services affecting the running of the company.

Details of departure times, estimated arrival times, passenger handling problems, defects affecting the aircraft and crew rostering are the main items dealt with.

Some of the expressions used by aircrew using 'company' frequencies are explained in the following paragraphs. Most are straightforward language, in English, but often foreign pilots will be heard speaking in their native tongue.

Departure and Arrival Information

Pilots of different nationalities often give this information in different forms, but the usual method is in three parts:

(i) Clearance to start engines (often quoted as 'push-back' indicating that the aircraft has been pushed backwards away from the docking gate);

(ii) Take-off time;

(iii) Estimated time of arrival at destination.

These times are separated by oblique lines (for example 08.20/08.33/11.45) referred to as 'oblique', 'diagonal', 'stroke' or 'slash' (American). In this example, the message would be *'Pushed at zero eight two zero, diagonal zero eight three three, estimate Palma one one four five, delay due to ATC.'*

Alternatively:

'Off blocks zero eight two zero stroke zero eight three three, ETA Palma one one four five, delay due to ATC.'

Passenger Information

Information on passengers is usually included. The word passengers is often abbreviated to 'PAX'. A 'full house' means that the seats are all occupied. The total number of fare-paying passengers is given, followed by the number of non-fare paying infants and babies (or 'YPs' — young persons) — for example, *'two three five plus two on board'*. Infants are also sometimes described as 'tenths', for example, *'two tenths'* or even in decimals! — for example, *'two three five point two pax'*.

Crew information is occasionally given, with the number of persons on the flight deck followed by the number in the cabin, eg *'Crew two plus four, Captain Johnson'*.

Unaccompanied children (or minors) are mentioned to alert the airport personnel that special care will be needed. Similarly, elderly people often required special considerations.

Wheelchairs are provided at many airports for persons who may find difficulty in managing the walk from the aircraft to the terminal. Some people, of course, need a wheelchair permanently and usually it will be carried in the hold of the aircraft.

Requests for wheelchairs are commonplace with a distinction between passengers who are unable to walk off the aircraft ('lift-off wheelchairs') and those who can ('walk-off wheelchairs').

Aircraft Defects
Defects on the aircraft are one of the items heard most often in company messages. Sometimes they are explained in plain language, but a few airlines prefer their crews to describe defects by reference to a technical manual which specifies the particular faults. In such cases the defects are given only as a series of reference numbers.

An 'Allowable Deferred Defect' (ADD) is a fault which does not require immediate attention.

Where external ground power is required a Ground Power Unit (GPU) will be requested.

A Technical Stop (referred to usually as a 'Tech Stop') is when a flight finds it necessary to make an intermediate stop en route, usually for taking on additional fuel or possibly for a crew change. Also, a flight which is unable to continue to its destination airport because of poor weather may land at an intermediate point in order to wait for an improvement in the conditions at the destination. If the tech stop is of short duration, the passengers would normally remain on board during the turnaround.

Most of the operational details concern refuelling, reasons for delay, crew placing, refreshments for the crew, bar stocks, personal messages for crew and passengers and other general matters — even the latest football score!

'Selcall' frequency details are also included by some airlines. (See Chapter 7.)

The parking bay at the airport is referred to as either the 'stand' or the 'gate'.

12 Radio Frequency Allocation

VHF Radio Frequencies
The following list gives VHF radio frequencies in use for controlled airspace and the Special Rules Area for the United Kingdom.

The list relates to airways which can be identified on radio navigation charts.

Where more than one frequency is given, the first is the one most likely to be in use; the others are used as directed by ATC.

At the end of the airways lists are a few general frequencies which may also be of use.

Military airfields may often be heard on VHF, in contact with civilian traffic in the area, or handling military flights intending to enter controlled airspace. All other traffic operates on UHF military frequencies and cannot be received on a VHF set.

	Area	Callsign	Frequency
Amber 1	Skipness to Prestwick	Scottish Control	124.9
	Prestwick to 54°30'N	Scottish Control	126.25 124.9
	54°30'N — Stafford	London Control	131.05 132.7
	54°34'N to Pole Hill	Manchester Control	126.65 124.2
	Stafford to abm Woodley	London Control	133.7
	S of Woodley to FIR bdy	London Control	127.7
Amber 1 East	Pole Hill to Lichfield	London Control	131.05 132.7
	Pole Hill to abm Birmingham	Manchester Control	126.65 124.2
	Lichfield to Woodley	London Control	133.7 134.75
	S to Woodley to FIR bdy	London Control	127.7 135.05

Area		Callsign	Frequency
Amber 2	Pole Hill to Lichfield East	London Control	131.05 132.7
	Lichfield East to Woodley	London Control	133.7 135.25
	Pole Hill to abm Birmingham	Manchester Control	126.65 124.2
	Lichfield East to Brookmans Park	London Control	134.75 133.7
	S of Brookmans Park to FIR bdy	London Control	127.1 132.45
Amber 2 West	Within London FIR	London Control	127.1
Amber 25	Dean Cross to Rexham	London Control	128.05
	Dean Cross to Rexham	Manchester Control	133.05
	Rexham to Rhoose	London Control	131.2
	Rhoose to 50°N	London Control	132.6 129.2
	50° N to Southern Zone bdy	Jersey Zone	125.2
Amber 30	Within London FIR	London Control	127.1
Amber 34	Within London FIR	London Control	127.7
Amber 34 East	Within London FIR	London Control	127.7
Amber 34 W	Within London FIR	London Control	134.45 127.7
Blue 1	West of Wallasey	London Control	128.05
	West of Wallasey	Manchester Control	133.05
	Wallasey to Barton	London Control	128.05
	Wallasey to Barton	Manchester Control	125.1
	Barton to Ottringham	London Control	131.05 132.7
	Barton to Millbrook	Manchester Control	126.65 125.1
	East of Ottringham	London Control	134.25 127.95
Blue 2	East of Glasgow	Scottish Control	As directed by ATC
	Glasgow to FIR bdy	Scottish Control	124.9
Blue 3	Northwest of Stafford	London Control	128.05 129.1
	Whitegate to abm Birmingham	Manchester Control	125.1 124.2
	South of Brookmans Park to FIR Bdy	London Control	127.1 134.9
	Stafford to Brookmans Park	London Control	133.7 134.75
Blue 4	Brookmans Park to abm Birmingham	London Control	134.75 133.7
	Brookmans Park to Hucknall	London Control	134.75 133.7
	Abm Birmingham to Pole Hill	Manchester Control	126.65 124.2
	Hucknall to Pole Hill	London Control	131.05 132.7
Blue 29	Within London FIR	London Control	129.6 127.95
	South of Brookmans Park to FIR Bdy	London Control	127.1 134.9
Green 1	West of Chepstow	London Control	131.2
	Chepstow to Woodley	London Control	132.8 131.2
	E of Woodley to FIR bdy	London Control	134.9 127.1
Red 1	Entire Route	London Control	134.45 127.7 132.3
	South of Southampton	Southampton	121.3
Red 1 North	Within London FIR	London Control	129.6 127.95 133.45
Red 1 South	Within London FIR	London Control	129.6 127.95 133.45
Red 1 West	Entire Route	London Control	134.45 132.3 127.7
Red 3	West of Belfast	Scottish Control	124.9
	Belfast to Robin	London Control	128.05 129.1
	Belfast to Robin	Manchester Control	133.05 125.1
	South of Robin	London Control	135.25 133.7
Red 14	Entire Airway	London Control	131.2
Red 23	Entire Airway	Scottish Control	As directed by ATC
Red 25	Entire Route	London Control	127.7
White 7	Entire Airway	London Control	127.7
White 8	South of 50° N	Jersey Zone	125.2
	North of 50° N	London Control	127.7
White 9	Entire Airway	Scottish Control	128.5 124.9

	Area	Callsign	Frequency
White 17	50N to Midhurst	London Control	134.45 132.3 127.7
	Midhurst to Dover	London Control	134.9 127.1
White 22	Biggin — Abm Birmingham	London Control	134.75 133.7
	Abm Birmingham-Pole Hill above FL130	London Control	131.05 132.7
	Abm Birmingham-Pole Hill FL130 & below	Manchester Control	126.65 124.2
White 37	Wallesey-Sapcote above FL130	London Control	128.05 129.1
	Wallesey-Sapcote FL130 & below	Manchester Control	133.05 125.1
White 38	ORTAC to Sampton	London Control	134.45 132.3 127.7
	Sampton to NORRY	London Control	132.8 131.2
	NORRY to Westcott	London Control	133.7 134.75
White 39	Within London FIR	London Control	131.2

Lower ATS Advisory Routes Frequency Allocation

	Area	Callsign	Frequency
DA 1	Within Scottish FIR	Scottish Control	124.9 131.3
DB 22	South of Aberdeen	Scottish Control	124.5
	Aberdeen to Klondyke	Scottish Control	131.3 133.2
DB 40	Within London FIR	London Control	131.2
DG 4	Within London FIR	London Control	132.6
DG 27	North of Black Head Light	Scottish Control	126.25 124.9
(Western Sect)	South of Black Head Light	London Control	128.05 129.1
	South of Black Head Light	Manchester Control	133.05
DG 27	Above FL 130	London Control	128.05 129.1
(Eastern Sect)	FL 130 & below	Manchester Control	133.05
DR 8	Dawlish to Ibsley	London Control	132.6
	Ibsley to Sampton	London Control	134.45 132.3 127.7
DR 23	Within Scottish FIR	Scottish Control	124.5
DR 37	Within London FIR	London Control	132.6
DW 2	West of Fleetwood	London Control	128.05 129.1
	West of Fleetwood	Manchester Control	133.05
	East of Fleetwood	London Control	131.05
	East of Fleetwood	Manchester Control	124.2 126.65
DW 3	South of Inverness	Scottish Control	124.5
	Inverness to Sumburgh	Scottish Control	131.3 133.2
DW 4	Within Scottish FIR	Scottish Control	131.3 133.2
DW 5	Within Scottish FIR	Scottish Control	131.3 133.2
DW 6	Glasgow to Stornoway	Scottish Control	124.9
	Stornoway to Inverness	Scottish Control	131.3 133.2
DW 9	Within Scottish FIR	Scottish Control	124.5
DW 10	Within Scottish FIR	Scottish Control	124.9
DW 11	E of Dean Cross	Border Radar	132.9
		Scottish Control	128.5
	W of Dean Cross	London Control	128.05 129.1
	W of Dean Cross	Manchester Control	133.05

Upper ATS Routes Frequency Allocation

	Area	Callsign	Frequency
UA 1	North of Ambel	Scottish Control	135.85
	Ambel to abm Lichfield	London Control	131.05 132.7
	Abm Lichfield to abm Woodley	London Control	133.7
	S of Woodley to UIR bdy	London Control	127.7

Area		Callsign	Frequency
UA 1 East	Pole Hill to Lichfield	London Control	131.05
	Lichfield to Woodley	London Control	133.7 134.75
	S of Woodley to UIR bdy	London Control	127.7 135.05
UA 2	Dean Cross to Ambel	Scottish Control	135.85
	Ambel to Lichfield East	London Control	131.05 132.7
	Lichfield East to Brookmans Park	London Control	135.25 133.7
	S of Brookmans Park to UIR bdy	London Control	127.1 132.45
UA 2 West	Entire Route	London Control	127.1 132.45
UA 25	Dean Cross to 5430N	Scottish Control	135.85
	5430N to South of Wallasey	London Control	128.05 129.1
	S of Wallasey to S of Brecon	London Control	133.6
	S of Brecon to UIR bdy	London Control	132.6
UA 25 East	Pole Hill to Telba	London Control	131.05 132.7
	Telba to Exmoor	London Control	133.6
UA 30	Entire Route	London Control	127.1
UA 34	Wallasey to Telba	London Control	128.05 129.1
	Telba to abm Woodley	London Control	133.7
	Abm Woodley to UIR bdy	London Control	127.7
UA 37	South Fisher to 5230N	London Control	134.25 127.95
	5230N to Gabbard	London Control	129.6 127.95
UA 38	Within London UIR	London Control	133.6
UB 1	West of Wallasey	London Control	128.05
	Wallasey to Ottringham	London Control	131.05
	East of Ottringham	London Control	134.25 127.95
UB 3	North of Stafford West	London Control	134.75 133.7
	Stafford West to Brookmans Park	London Control	133.7 134.75
	Brookmans Park to Dover	London Control	127.1 134.9
UB 4	Talla to 54°30′N	Scottish Control	135.85
	54°30′N to Hucknall	London Control	131.05
	Hucknall to Brookmans Park	London Control	135.25 133.7
	S of Brookmans Park to UIR bdy	London Control	127.1 132.45
UB 5	Within London UIR	London Control	132.7 134.25
UB 10	Within London UIR	London Control	133.6
UB 13	North of Flamboro'	Scottish Control	135.85
	South of Flamboro'	London Control	134.25 127.95
UB 22	Entire Route	Scottish Control	135.85
UB 24	Within London UIR	London Control	134.25 127.95
	Within Scottish UIR	Scottish Control	135.85
UB 29	Woodley to abm Brookmans Park	London Control	133.6 132.8
	E of Brookmans Park to UIR bdy	London Control	129.6 127.95
UB 40	Entire Route	London Control	133.6 132.6
UG 1	W of Woodley to UIR bdy	London Control	133.6 132.8
	E of Woodley to UIR bdy	London Control	134.9 127.1
UG 4	Within London UIR	London Control	132.6
UG 11	Entire Route	Scottish Control	135.85
UR1, UR 1 N & UR 1 S	W of Lambourne, or abm Lambourne to UIR bdy	London Control	134.45 127.7 132.3
	E of Lambourne or abm Lambourne to UIR bdy	London Control	129.6 127.95 133.45
UR 1W	Entire route	London Control	134.45 132.3 127.7
UR 3	North of 5300N	London Control	128.05
UR 4	West of Pole Hill	London Control	128.05
	Pole Hill to Ottringham	London Control	131.05
	East of Ottringham	London Control	134.25 127.95
UR 8	50N 08W to Ibsley	London Control	132.6
	Ibsley to Sampton	London Control	134.45 132.3 127.7

	Area	Callsign	Frequency
UR8 S	Entire Route	London Control	132.6
UR 14	50N to Ibsley	London Control	134.45 132.3 127.7
	Ibsley to Boundary	London Control	132.6 133.6
UR 23	Within Scottish UIR	Scottish Control	135.85
UR 25	Entire Route	London Control	127.7
UR 37	West of Ibsley	London Control	132.6
	Ibsley to abm Midhurst	London Control	134.45 127.7 132.3
	East of abm Midhurst	London Control	134.9 127.1
UR 38	Entire Route	Scottish Control	135.85
UW 14	Entire Route	Scottish Control	135.85
UW 17	Entire Route	London Control	134.45 132.3 127.7
UW 38	ORTAC to Sampton	London Control	134.45 132.3 127.7
	Sampton to NURRY	London Control	132.8 131.2
	NORRY to Westcott	London Control	133.7 134.75
UW 39	Entire Route	London Control	133.6 132.6

Miscellaneous VHF Radio Frequencies

Emergency Frequency (MayDay'):	121.3
Volmet Main:	135.37
Volmet North:	126.6
Volmet South:	128.6
Shanwick Oceanic Clearances:	123.95
	127.65
Shanwick Organised Tracks:	133.80

Flight Information Service
Special Rules Area (above FL245)

London Control:	131.05 134.25 (North)
London Control:	132.6 (South)

London and Scottish FIR's

Scottish Information:	124.9
London Information North of B1:	134.7
London Information South of B1- East of A1	124.6
London Information South of B1- West of A1	124.75
Border Radar	132.9, 134.85
Midland Radar	132.25
Highland Radar	134.1
Amsterdam Control	125.75
Brussels Control	128.8, 131.1
France Control	129.0, 132.0, 132.12, 135.65, 133.47
Maastricht Control	132.2
Paris Control	125.7, 129.35
Shannon Control	124.7, 131.15, 135.6

Airfield	Approach	Tower	Ground
Aberdeen (Dyce)	120.4	118.1	
Aberporth	122.15	122.15	
Abingdon	120.9	130.25	
	134.3		
Alderney	128.65	123.6	
Belfast (Aldergrove)	120.0	118.3	
Benson	120.9	122.1	
	134.3		
Bentwaters	119.0		
	128.42	122.1	

Airfield	Approach	Tower	Ground
Biggin Hill	129.4	134.8	
Binbrook	125.35	122.1	
	132.25		
Birmingham	120.5	118.3	
	118.05		
Blackpool	118.4	118.4	
Boscombe Down	126.7	130.0	
Bournemouth	118.65	125.6	
Brawdy	122.1	122.1	
	124.4		
Bristol	127.75	120.55	
Bristol (Filton)	130.85	124.95	
Brize Norton	133.75	126.5	
	122.1		
Cambridge	123.6	122.2	
Cardiff-Wales	125.85	121.2	
Carlisle	123.6	123.6	
Chester	123.35	124.95	
Chichester (Goodwood)	122.45	119.7	
Chivenor	122.1	122.1	
	130.2		
Church Fenton	126.5	122.1	
	129.15		
Coltishall	125.9	122.1	
	122.1		
Coningsby	122.1	122.1	
	120.8		
Cork	119.9	119.3	121.8
		121.7	
Cottesmore	130.2	122.1	
	123.3		
Coventry	119.25	119.25	
Cranfield	122.85	123.2	
Cranwell	122.1	122.1	
	119.0		
Culdrose	134.05	122.1	
		123.3	
Dublin	128.0		121.8
	119.55	118.6	
	121.1		
Dunsfold	122.55	124.32	
	118.82		
East Midlands	119.65	124.0	121.9
Edinburgh	121.2	118.7	121.75
Exeter	128.15	119.8	
Fairford	119.0	122.1	
	122.1		
Farnborough	125.25	122.5	
Finningley	120.35	122.1	
Glasgow	119.1	118.8	121.7
Gloucester (Staverton)	125.65	125.65	
Greenham Common	UHF only	122.1	
Guernsey	128.65	119.95	
Halfpenny Green	123.0	121.95	
Hatfield	123.35	130.8	
Hawarden	123.35	124.95	

Airfield	Approach	Tower	Ground
Honington	129.05	122.1	
	128.42		
Humberside	123.15	118.55	
Inverness	122.6	122.6	
Isle of Man (Ronaldsway)	120.85	118.9	
Jersey	125.2	119.45	121.9
	120.3		
	118.55		
	120.45		
Kemble	122.1	122.1	
	123.3		
Lakenheath	129.05	122.1	
Leavesden	122.1	122.1	
	121.4		
Leeds/Bradford	123.75	120.3	
Leeming	132.4	122.1	
	122.1		
Leuchars	126.5	122.1	
Linton-on-Ouse	129.15	122.1	
Liverpool	119.85	118.1	
London (Heathrow)	119.2	118.7	121.9
	119.5	118.5	(Start up 121.7)
		121.0	(ATIS 121.85)
			(ATIS 133.7)
London (Gatwick)	119.6	124.22	121.8
		127.55	(Start up 121.95)
			(ATIS 121.75)
			(ATIS 117.90)
London (Stansted)	125.55	118.15	
	126.95		
Luton	129.55	120.2	121.75
	127.3		
	120.75		
Lydd	120.7	120.7	
		131.3	
Lyneham	123.4	122.1	
Machrihanish	125.9	122.1	
Manchester	124.2	118.7	121.7
	125.1		
	119.4		
Manston	126.35	124.9	
	123.0	126.35	
	122.1		
Marham	124.15	122.1	
Mildenhall	129.05	122.55	
Newcastle	126.35	119.7	
Northolt	134.15	134.15	
Norwich	119.35	118.9	
	122.1		
Odiham	125.25	122.1	
Oxford (Kidlington)	130.3	119.8	121.75
Plymouth	123.2	122.6	
Portland	124.15	122.1	
	122.1	124.15	
		123.1	
Prestwick	120.55	118.15	
St Athan	125.85	122.1	

Airfield	Approach	Tower	Ground
St Mawgan	126.5	123.4	
	122.1	122.1	
Scilly Isles	120.55	118.15	
Sculthorpe	UHF only	122.1	
Shannon	121.4	118.7	121.8
	120.2		
Shawbury	124.15	122.1	
Shobdon	123.5	123.5	
Shoreham	123.15	125.4	
Southampton (Eastleigh)	128.45	118.2	
	131.0		
	121.3		
	128.85		
Southend	128.95	119.7	
Swansea	119.7	119.7	
Tees-side	118.85	119.8	
Upper Heyford	123.3	122.1	
	128.55		
Valley	134.35	122.1	
Waddington	127.35	122.1	
Wattisham	123.4	122.1	
	128.42		
Weston	129.25	122.5	
Wethersfield	UHF only	122.1	
Wick	119.7	119.7	
Wittering	122.1	122.1	
Woodbridge	UHF only	119.15	
		122.1	
Wyton	134.05		
	128.42	122.1	
Yeovil	130.8	125.4	
Yeovilton	127.35	122.1	

Useful Addresses

Air Traffic Control Centres

London Air Traffic Control Centre, Porters Way, West Drayton, Middlesex UB7 9AX. Tel: 0895-445566

Scottish and Oceanic Air Traffic Control Centre, Atlantic House, Sherwood Road, Prestwick, Ayrshire KA9 2NR. Tel: 0292-79800

Main Organisations

National Air Traffic Services, CAA House, 45-49 Kingsway, London WC2B 6TE. Tel: 01-379 7311

Civil Aviation Authority, CAA House, 45-59 Kingsway, London WC2B 6TE. Tel: 01-379-6311
(The CAA Library, which is open to the public, is located at CAA House, Kingsway.)

British Airports Authority, 2 Buckingham Gate, London SW1E 6JL. Tel: 01-834 6621

British Airways, Speedbird House, London Heathrow Airport, Hounslow, Middlesex TW6 2JA. Tel: 01-759 5511

Eurocontrol, Rue de la Loi 72, 1040 Brussels, Belgium

Training

International Aeradio Ltd, Bailbrook College, London Road West, Bath, Avon BA1 7JD. Tel: 0225-858941

College of Air Traffic Control, National Air Traffic Services, Bournemouth (Hurn) Airport, Christchurch, Dorset BH23 6DF. Tel: 0202-472334

Charts and Publications

British Airways (Aerad), Customer Services, Aerad House, PO Box 10, Heathrow Airport, Hounslow, Middlesex TW6 2JA. Tel: 01-562-0795

CSE Aviation (Jeppesen agents), Oxford Airport, Kidlington, Oxford OX5 1RA. Tel: 08675-4321

Non-UK Enquiries: Jeppesen & Co GmbH, PO Box 16-447, D-6000 Frankfurt-Main, F.R. Germany

Royal Air Force, No 1 AIDU, RAF Northolt, West End Road, Ruislip, Middlesex HA4 6NG. Tel: 01-845-2300 Extension 209

Civil Aviation Authority, Aeronautical Information Service, Tolcarne Drive, Pinnor, Middlesex HA5 2DU. Tel: 01-866-8781

Civil Aviation Authority, Printing & Publishing, Greville House, 37 Gratton Road, Cheltenham, Glos GL50 2BN. Tel: 0242-35151

Messrs Edward Stanford Ltd, 12-14 Long Acre, London WC2E 9LP. Tel: 01 836 1321

International Aeradio, Merchandising Service, Aeradio House, Hayes Road, Southall, Middlesex UB2 5NJ. Tel: 01 843 2411 Ext 494

Airtour International, Elstree Aerodrome, Elstree, Hertfordshire WD6 3AW. Tel: 01 953 4870

Aircraft Owners & Pilots Association, British Light Aviation Centre, 50a Cambridge Street, London SW1V 4QQ. Tel: 01 834 5631

CAA Chart Room, Room T308, CAA House, 45-49 Kingsway, London WC2B 6TE. Tel: 01 379 7311 Ext 2569

Radios, Aerials, Information, Books

Aero Hobby Supplies, NCP Building, Air Cargo Centre, Birmingham International Airport B26 3QT. Tel: 021-782-8704

Lowe Electronics Ltd, Chesterfield Road, Matlock, Derbyshire DE4 5LE. Tel: 0629-2430, 2817, 4057, 4995

Waters & Stanton, 18 Main Road, Hockley, Essex. Tel: 0702-206835

Fairbotham & Co., 58-62 Lower Hillgate, Stockport, Cheshire. Tel: 061-480-4872

Edward Stanford, 12-14 Long Acre, London. WC2E 9LP. Tel: 01-836-1321

C5 at Heathrow, Unit 224, Norwood Cresent, London Heathrow Airport, Hounslow, Middlesex TW6 2EN. Tel: 01-759-3626

The Aviation Hobby Shop, 4 Horton Parade, Horton Road, West Drayton, Middlesex UB7 8EA. Tel: 08954-42123

Airtour International, Elstree Aerodrome, Hertfordshire. Tel: 01-953-4870

Aviation Data Centre, Unit Four, Browells Lane, Feltham, Middlesex TW13 7EQ. Tel: 01-890-8933

Miscellaneous

Servisair Ltd., Servisair House, PO Box No 22, Bramhall, Stockport, Cheshire SK7 2DA. Tel: 061-440-0044

ABC World Airways Guide, World Timetable Centre, Church Street, Dunstable, Beds. Tel: 0582-600111

Airlines

In this chapter the majority of civil airlines and military organisations using UK airspace are listed. In most cases the call sign used by ATC incorporates the carrier's name. There are, however, some exceptions, the most popular of which are British Airways ('Speedbird') and Pan American ('Clipper'). The call sign usually includes a two, three or four figure number. Most airline timetables give flight call signs, and a few also list their services in numerical order, which is especially useful for quickly identifying particular flights.

Timetables are frequently revised and it is difficult to keep completely up-to-date. Also, flights which do not stop in the UK may not be shown in local schedules. In a few cases, certain scheduled flights from Europe to the USA do land in the UK, but the flight number for both parts of the journey is the same even though there may be a change of aircraft type. Naturally it is impossible to guarantee that such a list is up-to-date by the time it is published. New airlines do come on to the scene, and unfortunately some may also go out of business. Nevertheless, the list will serve as a good basic guide for traffic using UK airspace and it is surprising how quickly the majority will be heard on the air. The following carriers can be heard in the UK airspace. The name of the organisation is given first, followed by the commonly used call sign.

Airline	Call sign
Aeroflot	Aeroflot
Aeromexico	Air Mexico
Aer Lingus	Shamrock
Air Algeria	Air Algeria
Air Atlantique	Air Atlantique

Airline	Call sign	Airline	Call sign
Air Bahama	Air Bahama	Business Aircraft	
Air Berlin	Air Berlin	Users' Association	Bizair
Air Bridge	Air Bridge	CAA Flying Unit	Minair
Air Canada	Air Canada	Calair	Caljet
Air Charter (Scotland)	Scotair	Canadian Military	Canadian Military
Air Charter & Travel	Actair	Capitol	Capitol
Air Commuter	Aircom	Cargolux	Cargolux
Air Ecosse	Air Ecosse	Caribbean	Caribbean
Air Europe	Air Europe	Cathay Pacific	Cathay
Air Express	Air Express	Cecil Aviation Ltd	CIL
Air France	Air France	Centreline Air	
Air India	Air India	Services Ltd	Centreline
Air Jamaica	Air Jamaica	Channel	Channel
Air Kilroe Ltd	Kilro	Civil Aviation Admin.	
Air Lanka	Air Lanka	of China	China
Air Lift	Airlift	Condor	Condor
Air London	Air London	Continental	Continental
Air Malta	Air Malta	CP air	Empress
Air Mauritius	Air Mauritius	CSA	CSA or
Air New Zealand	Air New Zealand		Czechoslovakian
Air Portugal	TAP or Air Portugal	Cubanair	Cubanair
Air UK	Ukay	Cyprus	Cyprus
Air Zimbabwe	Zimbabwe	Dan Air	Dan Air
Airwork Services		Delta	Delta
Training	Airwork	Eagle Flying Services	
Air Yemeni	Air Yemeni	Ltd	Eagle
Air Zaire	Air Zaire	Eastern	Eastern
Alia Royal Jordanian	Jordanian	Egyptair	Egyptair
Alidair	Alidair	El Al	El Al
Alitalia	Alitalia	Ethiopian	Ethiopian
American	American	Euroair	Euroair
Arrow	Arrow or Big A or	Euroflite Ltd	Euroflite
	Juliet Whisky	Evergreen	Evergreen
Austrian	Austrian	Express Air Service	Expressair
Aviaco	Aviaco	Fairflight Ltd	Fairflight
Avio Genex	Juliett Juliett	Federal Express	Federal Express
Balair	Balair	Finnair	Finnair
Balkan	Balkan	Flying Tiger	Flying Tiger
Bangladesh	Bangladesh	Ford Motor Co	Fordair
Beecham Group Ltd	BeechAir	Genair Ltd	Genair
Belgian Air Force	Belgian Air Force	German Air Force	German Air Force
Birmingham		Ghana	Ghana
Executive Airways	Birmex	Gibraltar	Gibair
Britannia	Britannia	Global	Global
Bristow Helicopter		Guernsey	Guernsey
Group	Bristow	Gulf Air	Gulf Air
British Air Ferries	Air Ferries	Gulfstream	Gulfstream
British Air Ferries		Hapaglloyd	Hapaglloyd
Business Jets Ltd	Bafjet	Hawaiian Air	Hawaiian
British Airtours	Beatours	Heavy Lift	Heavy Lift
British Airways	Speedbird	Iberia	Iberia
British Airways		Icelandair	Iceair
Shuttle	Shuttle	Inex Adria Avio	
British Caledonian	Caledonian or B-Cal	Promet	Juliett Papa
British Island Airways	British Island	Intercity	Intercity
British Midland	Midland	Iranair	Iranair
Brymon	Brymon	Iraqui	Iraqui

Airline	Call sign	Airline	Call sign
Irish Air Corps	Irish Air Corps	Sierra Leone	Sierra Leone
Israeli Air Force	Israeli Air Force	Singapore	Singapore
Italian Air Force	Italian Air Force	South African	Springbok
Itavia	Itavia	Spacegrand Aviation	Spacegrand
Janus Airways Ltd	Jan	Spantax	Spantax
Japan	Japan	Sudan	Sudan
Jat Jugoslav Airlines	Jugoslav	Swissair	Swissair
Jersey	Jersey	Syrian Air	Syrian
Jetstar	Jetstar	Tarom	Tarom
Kenya	Kenya	Thai	Thai
Kite	Kite	Tradewinds	Tradewinds
KLM	KLM	Transamerica	TransAmerica
Korean	Korean	Trans World Airways	TransWorld or TWA
Kuwait	Kuwait	Trinidad & Tobago	
Libyan	Libyan	Airways	West Indian
Loganair	Logan	Tunis	Tunis
London European	London European	Uganda	Uganda
Lot	Lot	United	United
Lufthansa	Lufthansa	UTA	UTA
Luxair	Luxair	Varig	Varig
Maersk Air	Maersk	Viasa	Viasa
Malaysian	Malaysian	Vickers	Vickers
Malev	Malev	Viking	Viking
Manx	Manx	Virgin	Virgin
Martinair	Martinair	Vernair (Vernons	
McAlpine Ltd	Macline	Pools)	Vernair
Metropolitan	Metropolitan	Wardair	Wardair
Middle East	Middle-east	Western	Western
Military Aircraft		World	World
Command (USA)	Mac	Worldways	Worldways
Monarch	Monarch	Yemen Airways	Yemen
Montana	Montana	Zaire	Zaire
Nation Air	Nationair	Zambia	Zambia
National	National		
Nigerian	Nigerian		
NLM	City		
Northwest	Northwest		
Olympic	Olympic		
Orion	Orion		
Pacific Western	Pacific Western		
Pakistan	Pakistan		
Pan American	Clipper		
People Express	People		
QANTAS	Qantas		
Quebecair	Quebecair		
Romanian	Romanian		
Royal Air Force	Rafair		
Royal Air Force			
Transport	Ascot		
Royal Air Maroc	Air Maroc		
Royal Navy	Navair		
Ryanair	Ryanair		
Sabena	Sabena		
Sam	Sam		
SAS Scandinavian	Scandinavian		
Saudi	Saudi		
Short Bros	Short		

I would like to record my gratitude once again for the advice and assistance given by the following people during the preparation of the first and second editions of this book: *D. Adams*, Manchester International Airport; *R. Beale*, Heathrow; *R. C. Brown*, SCATCC; *C. Buttars*, International Aeradio, Bath; *E. J. Burns*, Heathrow; *R. Cheyne*, Eurocontrol; *J. Ellis*, Servisair, *G. Gill*, International Aeradio, London; *M. Hundleby*, Manchester International Airport, *W. A. Jellet*, LATCC; *A. R. Latham*, Jeppesen; *R. E. G. Parfitt*, International Aeradio, Bath; *P. Perry*, Manchester International Airport; *D. W. Ward*, Eurocontrol; *J. Willis*, Servisair; *J. West*, Marconi.

In addition the following organisations also provided invaluable help: Aerad, British Airways, CAA, CSE Aviation; Lowe Electronics; Ministry of Defence, NATS, RAF.